A YOUNG PATRIOT

The American Revolution
as Experienced by
One Boy

☆

A YOUNG PATRIOT

The American Revolution as Experienced by One Boy

☆

by Jim Murphy

ILLUSTRATED WITH PRINTS

CLARION BOOKS
NEW YORK

Clarion Books
a Houghton Mifflin Company imprint
215 Park Avenue South, New York, NY 10003
Text copyright © 1996 by Jim Murphy

Text is 13.5/17-point Bulmer
Book design by Carol Goldenberg

Library of Congress Cataloging-in-Publication Data.

Murphy, Jim, 1947–
A young patriot: the American Revolution as experienced by one boy / by Jim Murphy.
p.   cm.
Includes bibliographical references (p.   ).
ISBN 0-395-60523-7   PA ISBN 0-395-90019-0
1. Martin, Joseph Plumb, 1760–1850.   2. Connecticut—History—
Revolution, 1775–1783—Juvenile literature.   3. United States—
History—Revolution, 1775–1783—Campaigns—Juvenile literature.
4. Soldiers—Connecticut—Biography—Juvenile literature.
[1. Martin, Joseph Plumb, 1760–1850. 2. Soldiers. 3. Connecticut—
Revolution, 1775–1783—Campaigns.] I. Title.
E263.C5M366   1995
973.3'446—dc20   93-38789
[B]   CIP   AC

MP 10 9 8 7 6 5

*Frontispiece: George Washington (mounted on white horse) looks on as the
Declaration of Independence is read to the American troops in New York,
July 9th, 1776.*

For Laura, Bruce, and Jake—
proud residents of historic New York City

☆ ☆ ☆ ☆ ☆

Acknowledgments and Picture Credits

☆ ☆ ☆ ☆ ☆

I would like to acknowledge the following institutions for their generous help in locating source materials and pictures: the New Jersey Historical Society in Newark; the New Jersey State Library in Trenton; the Rutgers University Library in New Brunswick, New Jersey; and the Newark Public Library. Special thanks go to Alan Stein, Archivist for the Morristown National Historical Park.

Photo credits: frontispiece, pp. 15, 18—*Harper's Magazine; facing* p. 1, pp. 27, 37, 39 *top*, 52, 57, 77, 80, 85—National Archives; pp. 3, 4, 11, 12, 23, 41, 58, 59, 62, 79—Library of Congress; pp. 5, 8, 9, 16, 19, 21, 22, 25, 26, 29, 32, 39 *bottom*, 42, 44, 46, 48, 54, 55, 64, 65, 66, 68, 72, 76, 82—Author's collection; pp. 34, 86, 88—*Harper's Weekly*

Contents

☆ ☆ ☆ ☆ ☆

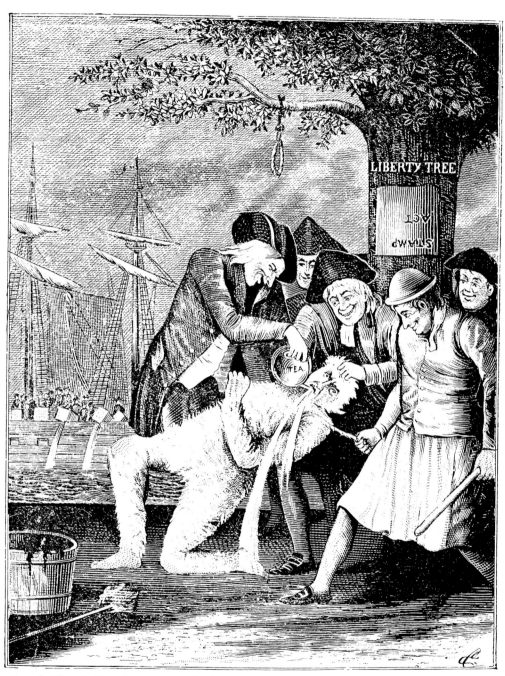

Joseph Plumb Martin grew up during a time of increasing anger with the British government. This 1774 British cartoon shows how a government agent trying to enforce the Stamp Act tax was forced to drink tea after being tarred and feathered. In the background, tea is being dumped into Boston Harbor.

CHAPTER ONE

The Smell of War

J oseph Plumb Martin was born on November 21st, 1760, in the tiny Massachusetts village of Becket. His mother, Susanna Plumb Martin, was the daughter of a wealthy Connecticut farmer, while his father, Ebenezer Martin, was the minister of Becket's Congregational church.

The Martins had lived very happily in Becket for six years, when Ebenezer suddenly lost his job. His impulsive nature and unorthodox opinions had upset a number of important parishioners. He had been, the church fathers would record, "an able, but not always *wise* man, one who said smart things and *odd* things that were remembered sometimes to his discredit and harm."

It would take nearly four years before Ebenezer found another church position, this one in Ashford, Connecticut. Sadly, as money ran low, the only choice Joseph's parents had was to leave their boy with Susanna's parents, who were living in Milford, Connecticut, nearly seventy miles away.

Despite the separation from his parents, Joseph seems to have flourished under his grandparents' care. He was especially attached to his grandfather. "For good he was, particularly to me," Joseph recalled fondly. "He was wealthy, and I had everything that was necessary for life. . . . It is true my grandsire kept me pretty busily employed, but he was kind to me in every respect, always gave me a playday when convenient, and was indulgent to me almost to a fault."

There are no pictures of Joseph and no descriptions of what he looked like. Judging from the chores he did around the farm and the many physically difficult assignments he received while in the army, he grew up tall, very strong, and possessed of an unlimited supply of energy.

We have a much clearer idea of his personality, mainly because of his extensive writings and through recollections of people who knew him. Joseph was unfailingly cheerful and outgoing, the sort of person who made friends easily and who liked to talk, a habit that sometimes got him (like his father) into hot water with those in charge. His adventurous spirit often led him into dangerous situations, but it never seems to have dulled his curiosity or fascination with the world around him. And while his words were often laced with humor and sarcasm, he had a thoughtful, caring side as well. On several occasions during battles he placed himself at serious risk in order to help wounded fellow soldiers.

Joseph was just four years old in 1764 when the British government passed the Sugar Act (to tax sugar, indigo, coffee, pimento, wine, and textiles) and the Currency Act (which required that the taxes be paid in silver and not in American paper money). Britain had exhausted its treasury fighting the French and Indian War (1754–1763) and wanted the colonies to pay for the military force still in America.

For their part, the colonies saw no need for the British army or the taxes. In 1765, a very determined King George III and his Parliament struck again, this time passing a Stamp Act (to tax all legal documents, newspapers, playing cards, and dice). King George was twenty-seven years old at the time, headstrong and convinced that his power to rule came directly from God. "The Colonies must either submit or triumph," he would later tell one of his ministers. "I do not wish to come to severer measures, but we must not retreat." He then ordered that "every means of distressing America" be applied until his foolish subjects "felt the necessity of returning to their duty."

Americans responded with more than anger. They took action: A group named the Sons of Liberty was organized, made up of men prepared to fight the Stamp Act "to the last extremity." At their urging, merchants refused to import British goods, most people stopped doing any business that required a stamp, and local stamp distributors were forced to resign. By putting unified economic pressure on England, the colonists hoped to make King George and Parliament relent in their efforts to tax them.

Joseph was only vaguely aware that something important was happening around him. "I remember the stir in the country occasioned by the Stamp Act, but I was so young I did not understand the meaning of it."

When British troops fired on an unruly mob of Boston citizens, killing three and fatally wounding two others, it was immediately dubbed the "Boston Massacre." Paul Revere's engraving shows a line of British soldiers gunning down an unarmed and peaceful group of citizens. The rifle barrel firing from a window (to the left of the Custom House sign) was a complete fabrication.

A mid-nineteenth-century artist, Alonzo Chappel, did a more realistic version of the incident. His mob is armed and actively attacking the soldiers. John Adams, patriot and future President of the United States, successfully defended the soldiers at their murder trial. Adams referred to the mob as "a motley rabble of saucy boys, negroes and molottoes, Irish teagues and outlandish jack tarrs."

It wasn't until William C. Nell's book The Colored Patriots of the American Revolution *appeared in 1855 that Black patriots were clearly portrayed. This version of the Boston Massacre features the mortally wounded Crispus Attucks.*

Joseph would grow up side by side with the increasingly angry discontent of the colonists. No sooner had the Stamp Act been repealed when a new series of taxes, the Townshend Acts, was issued on tea, glass, wine, oil, lead, and paint. Then, when he was nine, a rowdy gang of Boston civilians got into a quarrel with soldiers, resulting in the deaths of five Americans. No doubt the "Boston Massacre" was discussed heatedly throughout Milford: Joseph remembered that "my grandsire would talk with me about it while working in the fields, perhaps as much to beguile his own time as to gratify my curiosity."

Paying taxes of any sort to the King annoyed many people in the colonies, but that wasn't the only reason they rebelled against them. These laws were being passed by Parliament, a group in which Americans had no representation at all. There was no one there to voice their concerns or to guard their interests. For instance, these acts often chipped away at the personal freedoms of the colonists. One provision of the Townshend Acts allowed British officers to search anyone's home even without legal cause.

Joseph was thirteen when news of the "Boston Tea Party" reached Milford. In protest against the tax on tea, 150 Bostonians had stormed three ships and dumped the contents of 342 cases of tea into Boston Harbor.

The British responded quickly. First they closed Boston Harbor to all ships and imposed martial law on the city. To show their resolve and muscle, the British then moved nearly ten thousand soldiers into Boston. The colonies reacted in 1774 by calling the First Continental Congress. Fifty-two men from all of the colonies except Georgia met to condemn the British move and demand the repeal of the oppressive taxes. The most significant aspect of the meeting wasn't just that they stood up to the King and his government; it was that they stood up together.

As 1775 dawned, Joseph remembered that "the smell of war began to be pretty strong . . . [and] expectation of some fatal event seemed to fill the minds of most of the considerate people throughout the country."

CHAPTER TWO

Now I Was a Soldier

On the cool morning of April 21st, 1775, fourteen-year-old Joseph Plumb Martin got up before dawn as always and dressed for his long day of work. He ate a simple breakfast, then accompanied his grandfather to the field.

While young Joseph steered the plow through the hard, rocky soil, his grandfather walked alongside the horse, guiding it with the reins and urging it to keep moving. Whenever they hit a large stone, it was Joseph's job to dig it out and carry it to the side of the field. Joseph was tall for his age and very strong, so this work was fairly easy for him.

"All of a sudden," Joseph recalled, "the bells fell to ringing and three guns were repeatedly fired in succession down in the village."

Neither Joseph nor his grandfather had any idea why the signal was being given. It might be for some emergency, such as a barn fire, or simply to announce the arrival of a passenger coach. Joseph sensed something else. "I had some fearful forebodings. . . . The [British] regulars are coming in good earnest, I thought."

While his grandfather unhitched the horse and headed home, Joseph ran straight to Milford, which was about a mile away. A large number of people were gathered near the tavern to hear the news brought by an express rider from New Haven. Three days before, the rider told the crowd, approximately seven hundred British troops had left Boston at dusk and marched all through the night. The commander of British troops in North America believed the rebellious colonials had military supplies hidden in the little village of Concord and he wanted them seized.

Word of the approaching British had been spread throughout the countryside, mainly through the daring nighttime rides of William Dawes and Paul Revere. Local militia sent more messengers out with an urgent call to the farmer-soldiers to assemble and defend their homes. At dawn of the 19th, the British were still fifteen miles from Concord when they reached Lexington. But instead of a leisurely stroll through a sleeping town, the British found about sixty patriots lined up across the village green to challenge them.

A dashing Paul Revere warns a family about advancing British troops. Revere's part in spreading the news took center stage following the publication of Henry Wadsworth Longfellow's poem "Paul Revere's Ride."

Of course, many other individuals helped spread the word that night, most notably Ebenezer Dorr. Unfortunately, no one wrote a poem about Dorr, so he is usually portrayed as plodding along slowly.

No one really knew who fired the first shot. It might have been a nervous American alarmed at seeing a mass of red-coated soldiers advancing with bayonets fixed. What was known was that a shot was fired, followed by a few more; then the British halted to unleash a thunderous volley. Eight Americans fell dead and another ten were wounded.

After the surviving Americans fled, the British continued their journey to Concord where another bloody encounter took place near the North Bridge. The American defenders now numbered several hundred, but they were still no match for the highly organized lines of British troops. After a brief but spirited fight, the British were able to go about their search (but found very few military supplies). Their job done, the British headed back to the safety of Boston. By now, however, neighboring American militia had assembled along the road and took potshots at the retreating redcoats. When the British finally stumbled into Boston, they had lost two hundred fifty men, killed or wounded. American losses that day were forty-nine dead and forty-six wounded.

As the messenger was relating these events, the crowd in Milford grew increasingly upset and angry. In the past, the British government had forced them to pay unfair taxes and had restricted their rights through a series of bills they referred to as "the Intolerable Acts." Americans had been killed before, too, most notably at the Boston Massacre. But this new incident was something very different. The British had marched into the countryside and invaded helpless towns as if they were inhabited by criminals. No, the assaults on Lexington and Concord were nothing less than acts of war.

Volunteers were called to defend the area in case the British decided to march on Milford and a dollar was offered for the service. Joseph eyed the coin greedily, but did not step forward to sign his name to the list. He was worried that the adults would reject him because of his age and embarrass him in front of his friends. There was another even more important reason that held him back.

"I felt myself to be a real coward," he confessed. "What—venture my

British troops attempt to march back to the safety of Boston, while groups of American militia harass them from both sides with sniper fire.

This Alonzo Chappel painting captures the moment when a British charge at the Battle of Bunker Hill reaches the American line and hand-to-hand fighting breaks out.

carcass where bullets fly! That will never do for me. Stay at home out of harm's way. . . ."

So Joseph watched as a group of hometown volunteers—some of them boys his own age—went off to join American troops in New York.

If Joseph thought that the war would leave with these men and boys, he was mistaken. In May, news reached Milford that a band of two hundred Americans had crossed into Canada and captured Fort Ticonderoga, along with its valuable military supplies. This was followed a month later by the Battle of Bunker Hill.

Technically, the British won the Battle of Bunker Hill. They drove the fifteen hundred scrappy American defenders off and now held the land. But it had taken the British (then considered the best soldiers in the world) three assaults on the hill before they succeeded, something that surprised even them. More shocking was the human cost of the victory; of the twenty-five hundred British troops that took part in the battle, eleven hundred fifty were either killed or wounded. The American troops might not have looked like real soldiers, but they could be stubborn fighters.

Joseph heard many of the details of these encounters from American soldiers who stayed at his grandfather's farm during the winter. Not only did they describe what had happened, they often embellished their stories with heroic details. These stories fired Joseph's imagination and, as he confessed, began "to warm my courage."

By the time the spring of 1776 rolled around, Joseph had very nearly convinced himself of what he had to do. "By hearing the conversations and disputes of the good old farmer politicians of the times, I collected pretty correct ideas of the contest between this country and the mother country (as it was then called). I thought I was as warm a patriot as the best of them; the war was waged; we had joined issue. . . . I felt anxious . . . to be called a defender of my country."

Something else nagged at Joseph as well. The enlistments of his friends who had already gone off to war would soon expire. "They will come swaggering back, thought I, and tell me of all their exploits, all their 'hairbreadth 'scapes,' and [I] will not have a single sentence to advance. O, that was too much to be borne . . . by me."

If he needed added incentive, it's possible that the signing of the Declaration of Independence provided it. Congress adopted the Declaration on July 4th, and ordered the official printer to Congress, John Dunlap, to print eighty to one hundred copies of the document. The next day couriers were galloping along post roads and rural byways to deliver the call to freedom. A courier would have arrived in Milford late on the 5th or on the morning of the 6th, but Joseph made no mention of it or what he felt about its content.

His thoughts were on something much simpler—how long he wanted to serve as a soldier. The main American force, called the Continental Army, required the individuals who enlisted to serve for an entire year. Joseph had never lived away from home and had no idea what life in the army would be like for twelve months. "I did not like that. It was too long a time for me at the first trial; I wished only to take a priming before I took upon me the whole coat of paint for a soldier."

Fortunately, a call also went out for state troops, or levies, that asked only six months of service. This felt like a better length of time to Joseph, so on the evening of July 6th, he went to the enlistment station at the local tavern.

He did not tell his grandparents where he was going or what he intended to do. And he certainly did not ask their permission. While regulations stated that the minimum age for enlistment was sixteen, Joseph knew perfectly well that many fourteen- and fifteen-year-olds were being allowed to sign up. No, he would tell his grandparents after the deed was done and it was too late.

"Seating myself at the table, enlisting orders were immediately presented to me; I took up the pen, loaded it with the fatal charge [of ink], made several mimic imitations of writing my name, but took especial care not to touch the paper with the pen. . . ."

Even as he sat there, doubts filled his mind. While he had heard many daring tales of battle, he had also been told about the hardships. Food,

A young patriot is directed toward a Revolutionary recruiting office. Inside, a new recruit scribbles his name on the enlistment roster.

clothing, and ammunition were in short supply, enemy forces outnumbered the Americans and more redcoats were on the way, and many patriots had already been killed or badly wounded. He also worried that his going off would hurt his grandparents' feelings.

As he sat there, hesitating with the pen hovering an inch above the paper, one of his friends leaned over and nudged his hand. This "caused the pen to make a woeful scratch on the paper. 'O, he has enlisted,'" his friend said. "'He has made his mark; he is fast enough now.'"

"Well, thought I, I may as well go through with the business now as not. So I wrote my name fairly upon the indentures."

While his friends hooted their approval, Joseph sat back and stared at his signature. He remembered thinking, "And now I was a *soldier,* in name at least, if not in practice."

A boy marches off to war while a minister offers a prayer for his safe return.

CHAPTER THREE

The Smell of Powder

Once he'd signed the enlistment papers, Joseph began to worry about how he would tell his grandparents—and what their reaction would be. Legally, they could demand that his name be stricken from the papers and stop him from enlisting until he turned sixteen.

Joseph was surprised to discover that word of his enlistment had reached home before he did. "The old gentleman first accosted me with, 'Well, you are going a soldiering then, are you?'" It was painfully obvious to Joseph that his desire to leave home hurt his grandfather deeply, so he could not even answer the question. Then, after several moments of awkward silence, his grandfather gave him his grudging consent: "I suppose you must be fitted out for the expedition, since it is so."

At the beginning of the war, soldiers were told to supply their own uniforms and arms, which meant they usually arrived in camp in the clothes they wore every day. An eighteen-year-old in the Massachusetts militia recalled that many soldiers wore uniforms that consisted of "a short frock made of pepper-and-salt colored cotton cloth like a common working frock . . . ; it was short and open before, to be tied with strings, pantaloons of the same fabric and color, and some kind of cap. . . ."

A few larger towns managed to put together uniforms that looked somewhat military, though this sometimes caused serious problems. A company from Connecticut, called the Governor General's Foot Guards, wore uniforms that looked so much like those of the British grenadiers that they were fired on by their own side.

George Washington (mounted on white horse) looks on as the Declaration of Indepen-
dence is read to the American troops in New York, July 9th, 1776.

Joseph left no description of his "uniform." Most likely he wore the loose-fitting pants and shirt he wore when hunting, and a pair of well-worn boots. In addition, he brought his own musket, powder horn, cartridge box, tinderbox with flint, a wooden water barrel, and a knapsack with a change of clothes. His grandmother supplied him with cakes and plenty of cheese, "not forgetting to put my pocket Bible into my knapsack."

Around the 10th of July, Joseph boarded a small boat and sailed for New York City, in and around which Washington had the main part of his army. All Joseph wrote about saying good-bye to his grandparents was that "they wished me well, soul and body. I sincerely thank them for their kindness and love to me, from the first time I came to live with them to the last parting hour."

Joseph's life changed the moment he arrived in New York City. He had been used to a quiet, rural life where his closest neighbor was a five-minute walk away. Now he found himself in a bustling port city with a population of over twenty-five thousand people. Washington had approximately nineteen thousand soldiers in the immediate area and at

When Joseph arrived in New York, he was greeted by this view of the city.

any time several thousand of them were stationed in the city, making it even more crowded and noisy.

More startling to young Joseph was what he was expected to do. He and his fellow American soldiers had signed on to drive the redcoats out of the country. But instead of fighting, they were "called out every morning at reveille beating, which was at daybreak, to go to our regimental parade . . . and there practice the manual exercise, which was the most that was known in our new levies. . . ."

Because the streets of New York were both narrow and crowded with business traffic, it's likely that soldiers gathered at a wooded area at the tip of the island, called the Battery, and on the empty lots that dotted the city during the eighteenth century. There they would march back and forth, starting, stopping, and turning at the shouted command of an officer. They also formed long, neat lines and practiced loading and shooting their rifles at an imaginary enemy advancing toward them (though with powder in short supply, they did not actually fire their weapons very much).

Extended marches were made up the city's widest street, Broadway, passing Trinity Church, St. Paul's Chapel, and King's College along the way. No doubt they attracted a crowd of curious spectators at first. A mile or so up Broadway, they would come to a tall wooden fortification, stretching from the Hudson River to the East River, that had been built in 1754 during the French and Indian War.

This wall marked the end of the city. Beyond it the blocks of two- and three-story homes and businesses disappeared, to be replaced by rolling farmland, orchards, and rocky woodlands. Here troops would do much the same as in the city—start, stop, and turn on command, or simulate firing at the enemy. Such dusty and seemingly pointless activity was not Joseph's idea of soldiering. On top of this, the army's unvarying diet of salt pork or boiled beef, hard bread, and boiled potatoes or turnips began to wear thin. "I was a stranger to such living," Joseph confessed sadly. "I began to miss grandsire's table. However, I reconciled myself to my condition as well as I could; it was my own seeking."

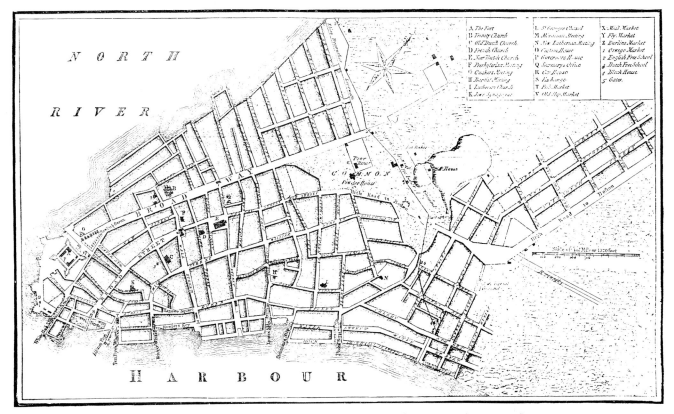

Joseph was stationed and did most of his training in lower Manhattan. This 1767 map shows the layout of the major streets.

For nearly two months, Joseph suffered the daily routine of army life. Homesickness soon gave way to boredom, and with it, mischief. "My levity . . . would often get the upper hand of me, do what I would; and sometimes it would run riot with me; but still I did not mean to do harm, only recreation, reader, recreation. I wanted often to recreate myself to keep the blood from stagnating."

Most such "recreation" was relatively harmless, such as oiling an officer's boots or filling a fellow soldier's canteen with vinegar. One incident, however, went beyond what might be considered a boyish prank.

It seems that Joseph and some of his friends discovered that a merchant near where they were staying had a cellarful of wine. One day they broke into the cellar and "liberated" the alcohol, passing flasks of wine out a window to any soldier who wanted them. Soon the street was filled with

Between June and August, 1776, over three hundred British ships anchored in the lower bay off Staten Island. Here landing parties of soldiers are rowing ashore to scout for campsites.

intoxicated and rowdy soldiers, and the owner of the wine was in a rage.

That's when General Israel Putnam arrived at the scene. Putnam was a short man with a bulldog face and a temper to match. In a scolding voice, he lectured those on the street about stealing civilian property and shaming the fight for freedom by such unsoldierly behavior. He ended by "threatening to hang every mother's son of them."

Joseph immediately ran to his room, where he had several bottles of wine under his bed. "[I] took a [drink] of the wine, and then flung the flask and the remainder of the wine out of my window, from the third story into the water cistern in the back yard, where it remains to this day for aught I know." A chastised Joseph added, "whether he was to be the hangman or not, he did not say, but I took every word he said for gospel. . . ."

Such interludes helped soldiers like Joseph get through the hot muggy days of summer. Then, on August 27th, the British attacked American forces on Long Island and Joseph's career as a soldier began in earnest. Not long after this news, orders arrived—Joseph and his company would go to Long Island to stop the advancing British troops.

None of this was particularly surprising. Between June and August, over three hundred British transport vessels and warships had arrived at Staten Island, bringing with them thirty-two thousand soldiers (eight thousand of whom were German Hessians) and ten thousand sailors.

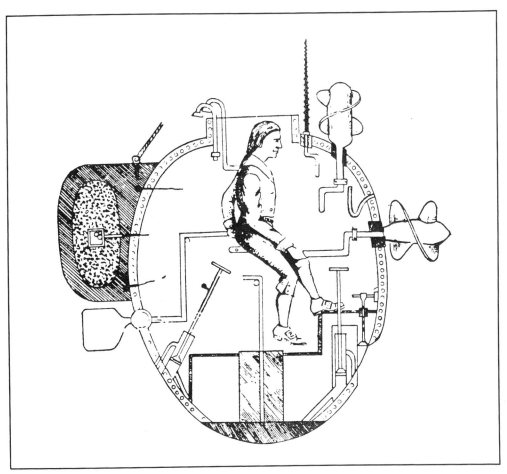

In September of 1776, the world's first combat submarine, "The Turtle," went into action. The machine, built by David Bushnell of Connecticut, managed to set off a bomb under the British flagship, the H.M.S. Eagle. The blast did little damage to the ship, but it did give the British a scare.

Everyone knew that the British forces were there and that eventually they would attack. Even so, Joseph confessed that hearing the actual orders "gave me a rather disagreeable feeling, as I was pretty well assured I should have to snuff a little gunpowder."

Joseph went to his room and packed his belongings. Before leaving, he went to the top of the house "where I had a full view of that part of the Island; I distinctly saw the smoke of the field artillery, but the distance and the unfavorableness of the wind prevented my hearing their report, at least but faintly. The horrors of battle then presented themselves to my mind in all their hideousness; I must come to it now, thought I."

Not long after this, the Connecticut soldiers were hustled down Maiden Lane and ferried across the East River to Brooklyn. "We now began to meet the wounded men, [a] sight I was unacquainted with, some with broken arms, some with broken legs, and some with broken heads. The sight of these a little daunted me, and made me think of home. . . ."

The sounds of battle were much louder and clearer, too, and Joseph's fear mounted. They halted briefly and Joseph nibbled away at a piece of sea bread. It was "hard enough to break the teeth of a rat," he remembered, and extremely salty, but gnawing it helped pass the tense minutes. When they resumed marching, it became apparent to Joseph that he wasn't the only one who was scared. One soldier had walked about a half mile before he realized he'd left his musket behind. Meanwhile, a lieutenant ran among the men "sniveling and blubbering, praying each [one of them] if he had aught against him, or if *he* had injured anyone that they would forgive him, declaring at the time that he, from his heart, forgave them if they had offended him. . . ."

Joseph could understand how a new soldier might show his fear, but not an officer. "Had he been at the gallows with a halter around his neck, he could not have shown more fear. A fine soldier you are, I thought, a fine officer, an exemplary man for young soldiers! I would have then suffered anything short of death rather than have made such an exhibition of myself."

Soon they came to the Gowanus Creek and its marshland, where

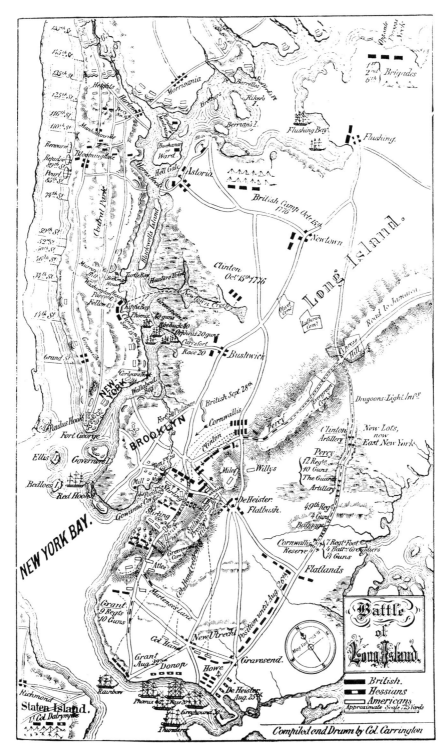

This 1876 map details ship and troop positions during the Battle of Long Island and subsequent action. Harlem Heights is near the top of the map.

General Lord Stirling (mounted in the center) and his troops are outnumbered and surrounded in heated action on Long Island.

Joseph had his first taste of battle. "A large party of Americans and British were engaged. By the time we arrived, the enemy had driven our men into the creek . . . where such as could swim got across; those that could not swim, and could not procure anything to buoy them up, sank."

The British soldiers formed a perfect line and unleashed a thunderous volley at the helpless soldiers floundering in the water. Seeing such a sight for the very first time produced shock and fear in many new soldiers. When powder in a musket was ignited, there was the crack of the explosion, followed by flames and billowing white smoke spitting from the front of the barrel and the flintlock. When fifty or sixty muskets were fired at the same time, it must have been like facing a terrifying fire-breathing demon.

Joseph had no time to be afraid. Orders were barked out, and his company began shooting at the British. Their firing was not very organized, but it was effective enough to make the enemy withdraw temporarily to regroup and reload. This allowed the Americans in the water to retreat safely, though without much dignity. "When they came out of the water and mud to us, looking like water rats, it was a truly pitiful sight. Many of them were killed in the pond, and more were drowned. Some of us went into the water after the fall of the tide, and took out a number of corpses. . . ."

Moments later the British reappeared, bringing along several cannons, and it was the Americans' turn to pull back.

As British soldiers advance, American troops break ranks and flee across the Gowanus Creek.

What Joseph had experienced was a tiny part of a much larger American retreat. Early on in the fighting on Long Island, Washington realized that his artillery and troops were too widely scattered to hold back the British. He decided to withdraw to Manhattan Island and make a stand there. At first, Washington intended to defend the entire island, but after several days he would reconsider. Such a plan would mean spreading troops the entire length of the island, leaving all sections vulnerable to a massed British attack. He decided, instead, to move his headquarters to Harlem Heights, where the terrain was steep and hilly and afforded a strong defensive position.

While the majority of the Americans scurried back to Manhattan and made their way to their assigned positions, Joseph and several thousand of the state levies were ordered to stay behind in Brooklyn. Washington hoped they could harass and hold up the British long enough to allow his forces to dig in at Harlem Heights.

"Our regiment was alone, no other troops being near where we were lying," Joseph remembered. The feeling of being abandoned increased when "a very heavy shower of rain . . . wet us all to the skin and much damaged our ammunition." Fortunately, the only times they had to fight redcoats were when they went looking for food. After one particularly savage encounter in which several soldiers were severely wounded, the Americans decided it was safer to go hungry.

Several days later, Joseph's regiment was ordered to return to New York City where they were to join the rest of the state levies. The storm that had drenched Joseph had made it impossible for British troop-ships to land on Manhattan Island. Unfortunately, it had also made American efforts to dig into Harlem Heights difficult. Until things were ready, Joseph and the other levies were to stay in the central part of Manhattan to slow any British advance.

After landing at New York City, his company marched four miles up the island to a tiny cove just above Kip's Bay. The British maneuvered ships into the East River opposite to where Joseph was, but did not send a landing force. Weeks went by with the edgy Americans watching the

Beaten American troops struggle to haul artillery and other heavy equipment aboard flatboats before escaping across the East River to Manhattan.

British. The armies were so close that every so often soldiers shouted to each other. "We had a chain of sentinels quite up the river, for four or five miles. . . . At an interval of every half hour, they passed the watchword to each other, 'All is well.' I heard the British on board their shipping answer, 'We will alter your tune before tomorrow night.'"

At daybreak the next morning, Joseph was relaxing in an old warehouse, reading some papers he'd found there. "[Then] there came such a peal of thunder from the British shipping that I thought my head would go with the sound." British warships were pouring round after round of cannon shot on the meager American forces. At such close range the cannonballs were ripping up large chunks of earth and tearing limbs from the trees.

"I made a frog's leap for the ditch and lay as still as I possibly could and began to consider which part of my carcass was to go first." Soon British troops boarded small boats and began paddling toward shore. The Americans, battered and dazed and inexperienced, did not even bother to fire at the landing forces. They did the wisest thing they could think of; they took to their heels in a disorganized retreat.

"In retreating we had to cross a level, clear spot of ground forty or fifty rods wide, exposed to the whole of the enemy's fire, and they gave it to us in prime order. The grapeshot and langrage flew merrily, which served to quicken our motions."

When this fighting began, Washington immediately rode toward the point of attack, only to be met by a stream of fleeing soldiers. He shouted orders to the men in an attempt to rally them, but they—and their officers—poured on past him. A Continental officer, Colonel George Weedon, was appalled by the uncontrollable nature of the levies. ". . . Though General Washington was himself present . . . they were not to be rallied, till they had got some miles. The General was so exasperated that he struck several officers in their flight, three times dashed his hat on the ground, and at last exclaimed, 'Good God! Have I got such troops as these?'"

Joseph was not a part of this group rushing past General Washington. In his panic, Joseph had headed west until he came upon two men from his company, one of them a neighbor from Milford. The three wasted no time in reorienting themselves and were soon hightailing it up the widest road on the east side of Manhattan, the Post Road that connected New York to Boston.

"We had proceeded but a short distance, however, before we found our retreat cut off by a party of the enemy stretched across the island. I immediately quitted the road and went into the fields, where there happened to be a small spot of boggy land covered by low bushes and weeds. Into these I ran and squatting down concealed myself from their sight.

Several of the British came so near to me that I could see the buttons on their clothes. They . . . soon withdrew and left the coast clear for me again."

An hour later, Joseph came out from his cover and found himself completely alone. It was an extremely hot and humid day, and he was faint from lack of sleep, water, and food. He struggled through the woods, heading north toward Harlem Heights.

After traveling a half mile, Joseph once again encountered his Milford neighbor, who was ill and vomiting. "I tapped him on the shoulder and asked him to get up and go on with me. 'No,' he said, at the same time regarding me with a most pitiful look. 'I must die here.' I told him he should not die there nor anywhere else that day if I could help it, and at length with more persuasion from me and some force I succeeded in getting him upon his feet and to moving on."

In the afternoon, a violent shower soaked them through. It wasn't until after the sun went down that Joseph finally located some familiar faces. "Our company all *appeared* to rejoice to see us, thinking we were killed or prisoners. I was *sincerely* glad to see them, for I was once more among friends."

Joseph was one of about three thousand of the levies who would eventually straggle back to Washington's defensive position in Harlem. The British would attack Harlem Heights, and the Americans would repulse the attack and drive the redcoats off. But this did not worry the British. Instead of attacking directly a second time, the British used their warships to move troops upriver above and behind the American defenses.

Once again, Washington was forced to divide his forces in order to deal with the new British positions. Joseph's company was sent to White Plains where they had a number of bloody encounters with the enemy. A series of fierce battles were fought throughout the area, and while the Americans managed to hold their ground against superior British forces, it was clear that sooner or later the enemy would win.

On November 15th the British attacked Fort Washington, the last forti-

After taking Fort Washington, British forces landed at Fort Lee and forced Washington and what remained of his army to retreat across New Jersey.

fication held by the Americans at the northern end of Manhattan Island. Washington, along with some of his generals, had been at the fort that morning, but had left before the attack began. It was a good thing. The American troops put up a strong defense, but were no match for the combined British and Hessian forces. Nearly three thousand Americans were forced to surrender that day.

Next the British sailed across the Hudson River and attacked Fort Lee, where the Americans had a large supply of guns, gunpowder, tents, and a variety of other military supplies. Washington and some two thousand troops barely escaped, managing to take along the powder but little else.

Washington and what was left of his army fled across New Jersey, with British troops at their heels. Their trail was littered with abandoned muskets, broken equipment, and exhausted soldiers willing to surrender. The situation looked so dire that the New Jersey militia played it safe and did not respond to a call to aid Washington. With winter coming on, it seemed as if the American cause was doomed to a frozen end.

Joseph was not a part of this flight. His company was still near White Plains, moving from place to place to avoid the enemy. He had lost his extra clothes during the hectic retreat from Kip's Bay; no new equipment or supplies had been issued since. Food was so scarce that his company abandoned their cooking pots during one exhausting march.

On a rainy night in late November, Joseph found himself in a long trench with fellow soldiers, watching a British encampment. Every so often, the British artillery fired at the Americans, which forced them to stay in the trench. "In the part where I happened to be stationed, the water before morning was nearly over shoes, which caused many of us to take violent colds."

Joseph grew so sick that the next day he was ordered to withdraw to where the baggage and the few remaining supplies were. He made a bed of dry leaves and nestled in it as well as he could. With no doctor to tend him, and no food or water, his condition worsened. Fortunately for Joseph, his six-month enlistment ran out on December 15th and he was able to begin the long walk home.

Joseph was not the only soldier leaving. Thousands of enlistments expired at the end of the year, and when this happened, soldiers packed up what little gear they had and simply went home. Very few of these soldiers would rejoin the fight. With only a trickle of new recruits on the way, it seemed as if Washington's army would melt away entirely. The situation was so bad that Thomas Paine would lament in his pamphlet *The Crisis*: "These are the times that try men's souls. The summer soldier and the sunshine patriot will, in this crisis, shrink from the service of their country."

A sniffling, coughing, and weary Joseph seemed to be a part of this movement to give up. "Here ends my first campaign. I learned something of a soldier's life—enough, I thought, to keep me home for the future."

This illustration of George Washington was based on a painting by Charles Willson Peale done at the end of the war.

CHAPTER FOUR

Marching, Watching, Starving, and Freezing

Joseph spent the first weeks following his return home caring for his illness and fattening up on good country food. When he'd regained his strength and when the weather permitted, he set out to see "the place of my boyhood, visit old acquaintance[s], and ramble over my old haunts." There was much talk about the Revolution, too, and many people expected the American army to surrender before spring. The British certainly did, anyway.

After driving Washington out of New York and chasing him across New Jersey and into Pennsylvania, the British halted military operations for the winter. They were perfectly aware of the wretched condition of Washington's army and knew that enlistments were expiring in December. Their enemy was powerless and would probably give up when the icy breath of winter arrived. If that didn't happen, it didn't really matter to the British. Come spring and they would annihilate whatever was left of Washington's ragtag army easily. The British were so confident that many officers, including some high-ranking commanders, went back to England for well-deserved vacations.

While we know now that this was a foolish move, at the time it seemed like sound military tactics. Eighteenth-century warfare was carried on under strict, though unwritten, "rules" designed to minimize the destruction of life and property. For instance, armies did not fight during the winter months. Getting supplies to soldiers was a tricky business even during good weather. In winter, a sudden blizzard could strand thousands of soldiers and threaten them with frostbite and starvation. It was also a general practice for one side to surrender as soon as it saw it could not win a battle or war. By not forcing the victor to expend a lot of needless blood, the loser hoped to get more lenient peace terms. Such "rules" made perfect sense and most countries followed them. Of course, most countries did not have George Washington commanding their army.

Despite his army's dismal performance in New York, the dwindling number of soldiers, and lack of supplies, Washington simply refused to admit he was beaten. He was confident that with time, training, and experience, his soldiers could outfight the British. But he was a realist, too. He knew that leaders and supporters of the Revolution had lost confidence in him and his army. The fact that the New Jersey militia had failed to come to his aid during the retreat was vivid proof of that. To revive confidence, he decided that a bold military move was needed—and to do this he had to break some of the "rules" of warfare.

After escaping to safety, Washington did not settle his remaining soldiers into winter camp. He spent several weeks resting his troops, during which time he personally tried to convince those whose enlistments were soon to lapse to stay on into January. Then on Christmas night he marched his troops toward Trenton where a large number of Hessian soldiers was stationed.

Another unwritten rule of warfare was that nighttime marching and fighting was not done. Soldiers could get lost in the dark or they might inadvertently fire on their own troops or innocent civilians. But Washington wanted to completely surprise the enemy, and what better way to do this than to attack at night. The fact that it was Christmas Day and a winter storm was raging only enhanced the chances that the Hessians would be indoors trying to stay dry and warm.

"It is fearfully cold and raw and a snowstorm setting in," Colonel John Fitzgerald noted as the American troops set off. "The wind is northeast and beats in the faces of the men. It will be a terrible night for the

One of the most famous and inaccurate images of the American Revolution was done by Emanuel Luetze in 1851. The boat is the wrong size and shape and it was poled across the river, not rowed. The flag shown was not used until later in the war, and a standing Washington would have tipped the boat over.

soldiers who have no shoes. Some of them have tied old rags around their feet; others are barefoot, but I have not heard a man complain. They are ready to suffer any hardship and die rather than give up their liberty."

This time, Washington's plan worked. Washington struck at the Hessian troops from one side, while General John Sullivan attacked from the other. Caught between two advancing forces, the Hessians "were frightened and confused," Fitzgerald reported happily, "for our men were firing on them from fences and houses and they were falling fast. Instead of advancing they ran into an apple orchard. . . . It was not long before [they] threw down their guns and gave themselves up as prisoners."

One thousand Hessians were taken prisoner. Among those killed was the commandant of the Hessian troops, Colonel Johann Rall. Only two weeks before, he had referred to the American army as "country clowns."

The British were enraged by Washington's move and sent a large force out to crush the upstart Americans. Washington and his army managed to slip away, this time defeating the British rear guard at Princeton along the way. After this, the British recalled their troops and went into winter camp to brood and plan. American forces also retired for the winter, though in a much happier mood. In the brief space of nine days, the fragile American forces had pulled off two stunning victories, taken valuable supplies, and, most important, revived American spirits.

This positive feeling carried over into the spring of 1777 and probably resulted in thousands of enlistments to the American cause. Joseph was among them. Putting aside any reservations he might have had, he signed on again in April, this time for the duration of the war.

Joseph and his fellow Connecticut soldiers did not join the main portion of Washington's army in New Jersey. Instead, they were positioned forty miles up the Hudson River at Peekskill, with very specific orders from General Washington: "We should on all Occasions avoid a general Action, or put anything to the Risque, unless compelled by a necessity, into which we ought never to be drawn."

For the next five months Joseph found himself constantly on the move. "[Our] whole time is spent in marches, especially night marches," he grumbled, "watching, starving, and, in cold weather, freezing and sickness. If [we] get any chance to rest, it must be in the woods or fields, under the side of a fence, in an orchard or in any other place but a comfortable one, lying down on the cold and often wet ground, and, perhaps, before the eyes can be closed with a moment's sleep, alarmed and compelled to stand under arms . . . to receive an attack from the enemy."

Washington and his forces were doing much the same thing down in New Jersey. Without really meaning to, Washington had created a new kind of fighting, which we now refer to as guerrilla warfare. In this sort

George Washington (mounted in center) rallies his troops during the Battle of Princeton.

British soldiers are mowed down by a volley of musket fire during the Battle of Princeton.

of war, the smaller army avoids any fight it can't win and, instead, uses hit-and-run tactics to pick away at the larger, better-supplied enemy. The objectives are simple: make the enemy pay a great deal of money to keep its troops supplied, and wear down the morale of its soldiers.

The British found this sort of fighting contemptible and cowardly. One British officer, Robert F. Seybolt, grumbled that "The rebels . . . were frequently very troublesome to us, and every foraging party that went out was pretty certain to have a skirmish with them. Besides which, they made a practice of waylaying single persons or very small bodies on the road and killing them from behind trees or other cover in a most savagelike manner. . . . When we showed any force, they disappeared."

The Americans turned out to be extremely good at this sort of fighting, and it did wear away at the British over the years. But in 1777, the British still had the upper hand.

First, the British under General John Burgoyne recaptured Fort Ticonderoga in July, after which he threatened to seize Albany, New York. If this happened, British ships would control the entire length of the Hudson River. Then, in late August, the British landed eighteen thousand soldiers at Elkton, Maryland, on Chesapeake Bay. The American capital and home to the Continental Congress, Philadelphia, was just thirty miles away. It was an easy target, but the British took weeks to organize themselves and march toward the city.

The fact that the British moved so slowly gave Washington time to pull together a force of twelve thousand and meet the enemy at Brandywine Creek. This time the outnumbered American troops did not break and run in the face of overwhelming odds. They listened to their officers, held their lines, maneuvered when ordered, and fought bravely. Unfortunately, Washington was badly outgeneraled by William Howe, the British commander. When Washington discovered he had been outflanked, he withdrew before his army was totally destroyed. The British entered Philadelphia unchallenged on September 26th, while the American Congress fled into the countryside.

While all of this was happening, Joseph and the rest of the Connecticut

American soldiers hold their line and fire on advancing British and Hessian soldiers at Brandywine Creek. Despite their gallant stand, Washington was outmaneuvered and the American forces had to withdraw.

British troops march past Independence Hall in Philadelphia following the defeat of the Continental Army at Brandywine Creek.

troops had been moved south into New Jersey. One night in early October when they returned to camp they were greeted by much activity. "The troops were all preparing to march. Their provisions (what they had) were all cooked, and their arms and ammunition strictly inspected and all deficiencies supplied. Early in the evening we marched in the direction of Philadelphia. We naturally concluded there was something serious in the wind."

The landscape they traveled through was a series of low, rolling hills and gentle farmland, which made marching easy. The October night, damp and cool, was refreshing, but as they neared Germantown, Pennsylvania, "a low vapor lying on the land . . . made it very difficult to distinguish objects at any considerable distance."

The British had about nine thousand soldiers at Germantown, while the Americans numbered twelve thousand. With such a clear numerical edge, Washington saw the coming battle as an opportunity to destroy a large portion of his enemy's army. To carry this out, he devised a complicated battle scheme that would allow him to completely encircle the British. Joseph's brigade would be positioned to strike from the north. A victory at Germantown would let Washington take his soldiers into winter camp with another spirit-lifting victory.

"At about daybreak," Joseph recalled, "our advance guard and the British outposts came in contact. The curs began to bark first and then [our] bulldogs. Our brigade moved off to the right into the fields."

On the other side of the field, about one hundred yards away, British soldiers took up position behind a rail fence. "We immediately formed in line and advanced upon them. Our orders were not to fire till we could see the buttons upon their clothes, but they were so coy that they would not give us an opportunity to be so curious, for they hid their clothes in fire and smoke before we had either time or leisure to examine their buttons."

The British had not expected the attack, but they had responded quickly. Reinforcements were sent to hold back the enemy, but the sheer number of Americans overwhelmed them.

"They soon fell back and we advanced. . . . The enemy were driven quite through their camp. They left their kettles, in which they were cooking their breakfasts, on the fires, and some of their garments were lying on the ground, which the owners had not time to put on."

The thick fog slowed the movement of American troops and the British were able to regroup and counterattack. Small bands of British infantry ghosted through the fog, unleashing a volley of musket fire, then retreating to quickly reload and repeat the attack. Smoke joined the fog to further reduce visibility, and the acrid smell of gunpowder grew thick. Despite the possibility for chaos and confusion, the Americans maintained control of the fighting. For a while.

"Affairs went on well for some time. The enemy were retreating before us, until the first division that was engaged had expended their ammunition. Some of the men unadvisedly calling out that their ammunition was spent, the enemy were so near that they overheard them, when they first made a stand and returned upon our people. . . ."

At this point the inexperience of both the American soldiers and their officers showed. Companies turned to retreat, saw shadows moving in the distance, and opened fire—not realizing that they were firing on their

Americans storm a British stronghold at Germantown.

own troops. Panic followed and the army began to dissolve, just as it had on Manhattan Island. Only the physical courage of Washington, who literally blocked the path of retreating soldiers and officers, stopped the retreat from becoming a rout.

"After the army had collected again and recovered from their panic, we were kept marching and countermarching, starving and freezing, nothing else happening, although that was enough. . . ."

Washington rallied his troops and managed to hold the British back, though he had lost the advantage. The battle went on fitfully throughout the day, with pockets of intense fighting breaking out here and there. In the end, Washington was able to say he'd fought the British to a draw, but it was a long way from the clear-cut, decisive victory he had hoped for. In fact, the best face Washington could put on the engagement was that it was "rather more unfortunate than injurious."

After the Battle of Germantown and weeks of intense skirmishing with the enemy, Joseph and several hundred other soldiers were ordered to Fort Mifflin, an island on the Pennsylvania side of the Delaware just below Philadelphia.

Although the British held Philadelphia, the Americans had blocked off the river at this point with two hastily thrown together "forts"—one Fort Mifflin and, on another island, Fort Mercer. The Americans also had several ships, including one frigate. The British first attacked Fort Mercer, but when they lost two warships they turned their attention on Fort Mifflin and its four hundred fifty defenders.

Fort Mifflin was nothing more than a muddy island with crudely erected log defenses. The British brought in six heavily armed warships, plus several armed barges, and pounded away at the fort for five straight days. The Americans could do very little, in part because they had no cannonballs for their thirty-two-pound cannon. Things were so desperate that Joseph recalled men actually running after enemy cannonballs that were often "seized before [their] motion had fully ceased and conveyed off to our gun to be sent back again to [their] former owners."

Despite a truly heroic stand in which over two hundred Americans

A tattered and weary American army struggles toward Valley Forge.

were killed, Fort Mifflin had to be abandoned. Oddly enough, the battle did not receive much attention at the time and, even today, rarely makes it into history books. The survivors of the ordeal were justifiably upset by the way their suffering and the deaths of their comrades were forgotten so quickly. "But there was little notice taken of it," Joseph said sadly, "the reason of which is, there was no Washington, Putnam, or Wayne there. . . . Great men get great praise; little men, nothing."

Soon after, Joseph's company rejoined what was left of the main army. November was rainy and chilly; most nights Joseph slept out in the open, wet and hungry. In December, temperatures dropped and snow began to fall. As they marched toward winter camp at Valley Forge, Joseph summed up the situation clearly: "We were now in a truly forlorn condition,—no clothing, no provisions and as disheartened as need be."

Joseph clutched his musket to his chest and leaned into the bitter wind. Exhausted, his eyes half-shut against the cold, he slipped on an icy rut and felt the sharp cowhide edge of his moccasin cut into his ankle. Valley Forge was twelve miles away, so he knew he had a long and painful march ahead of him.

"The army is now not only starved but naked. The greatest part were not only shirtless and barefoot, but destitute of all other clothing, especially blankets. . . . Hundreds of my companions had to *go barefoot,* till they could be tracked by their blood upon the rough frozen ground."

Washington felt much the same way. On November 30th two thousand enlistments had expired and the men had gone home. Since then, one-quarter of what remained of his army had been reported as unfit for duty owing to sickness and hunger. Desertions were increasing at an alarming rate, too. In a letter to his brother, Washington spoke candidly: "If every nerve is not strained to recruit the New Army with all possible expedition, I think the game is pretty near up. . . ."

The last few miles to Valley Forge were uphill and the weary men struggled to keep going. While riding along at the rear of his troops, Washington had seen the red tracks on the ice and snow. He asked an officer nearby about this and learned that the last issue of new shoes had run out long before most of the men received them.

"Poor fellows," Washington said, as he watched the barefoot men shuffle quietly past. "Poor fellows."

Exhausted soldiers warm themselves by the fire and think of the homes they left behind.

CHAPTER FIVE

Sending the Lobsterbacks Scurrying

The sun had set by the time they arrived at Valley Forge, a bleak, wooded hillside that would be their home for the winter. Most soldiers were too exhausted to pitch tents or mount a guard. They had just enough strength to build log fires and curl up next to them on the bare ground. Joseph did get his tent up, but discovered he had another problem.

"It was dark; there was no water to be found and I was perishing with thirst. I searched for water till I was weary and came to my tent without finding any."

He asked those around him if they had any water or knew where to find some. No was the answer to both questions. Just then, "two soldiers, whom I did not know, passed by. They had some water in their canteens which they told me they had found a good distance off, but could not direct me to the place as it was very dark. I tried to beg a draught of water from them but they [refused to give me any]. At length I persuaded them to sell me a drink for three pence, Pennsylvania currency, which was every cent of property I could then call my own. . . ."

When Joseph woke the next morning, orders had already been issued to the troops. Shelter was the most critical need just then, so the army was directed to build a city of tiny huts. Each hut had a door at one end and a fireplace at the other and was big enough to house twelve men.

Few of the soldiers were in any mood or physical condition to do such hard labor and this included Joseph. "I never heard a summons to duty with so much disgust before or since as I did that."

To motivate his troops, Washington offered a prize of twelve dollars to the group that finished its hut first. Because they already had a tent up, Joseph and his friends ignored the order and rested instead.

"I lay here two nights and one day and had not a morsel of anything to eat, save half of a small pumpkin, which I cooked by placing it upon a rock, the skin side uppermost, and making a fire upon it. [After] it was heated through I devoured it with as keen an appetite as I should a pie made of it at some other time."

Eventually Joseph and his tentmates joined the rest of the army in building a hut. Activity in camp was so intense that a visitor noted, "They appeared to me like a family of beavers: everyone busy; some carrying logs, others mud and the rest fastening them together."

By January 3rd, 1778, most of the huts—Joseph's included—were up and occupied.

This didn't mean that their winter stay was comfortable. Far from it. Roofs leaked, crudely built fireplaces belched smoke into the huts, and the only bedding was straw tossed across the damp dirt floors. Sickness constantly visited the soldiers: records indicate that over twenty-five hundred men—one quarter of the army—died at Valley Forge that winter.

Joseph's strong physical condition helped him avoid serious illness, though he did have some unpleasant times. To guard against a possible smallpox epidemic, the entire army was ordered to be inoculated. Inoculations were a primitive and dangerous procedure back then. The patient's skin had to be cut open and a lancet dipped in smallpox inserted. Generally, the inoculated person would contract a mild form of the disease and recover in a week or so.

Unfortunately, a good number of the men developed a severe case of smallpox and died a horrible death. If this wasn't scary enough, even getting a mild form of the disease often produced oozing boils near the spot of the inoculation, boils that could take weeks and even months to completely heal. Joseph recounts another one of the side effects of being inoculated.

"When I was inoculated [for] the smallpox I took that delectable disease, the itch. We had no opportunity, or, at least, we had nothing to cure ourselves with . . . [and when we] applied to our officers for assistance to clear ourselves from it, all we could get was 'Bear it as patiently as you can. . . .'"

Finally, Joseph and his cabinmates did what most Revolutionary War soldiers did—they turned to self-doctoring. They combined sulfur and tallow and heated the mixture till it began to boil. Next the hot mixture was slapped directly onto the parts of the body that itched. The gooey salve burned and blistered the skin on contact and gave off an overpowering stink. To make the cure as bearable as possible, the group mixed a batch of hot whiskey toddy, which Joseph confessed to using freely. "But we obtained a complete victory, though it had like to have cost some of us our lives." As if recalling the recent military failures at Brandywine and Germantown, Joseph added, "This was a decisive victory, the only one we had achieved lately."

Far more dangerous than the smallpox inoculations was the constant lack of food. During the days that followed their arrival at Valley Forge, what little flour and beef there was ran out. As stomachs began to growl from hunger, so did the soldiers. The surgeon for the Connecticut infantry, Dr. Albigence Waldo, recalled in his diary: "Provisions short. . . . Heartily wish myself at home, my Skin & eyes are almost spoil'd with continual smoke. A general cry thro' the Camp this Evening among the Soldiers, 'No Meat! No Meat!'—the Distant vales Echo'd back the melancholy sound—'No Meat! No Meat!'"

The situation grew so desperate that the simple chant turned to a threat: "No Meat, No Soldier." As the days went by, the complaint grew: "No Meat, No Coat, No Flour, No Soldier."

Washington was well aware of the wretched condition of his troops and their discontent. He sent out urgent requests to officials and citizens for supplies and food, carefully informing them that "for some days past,

By His EXCELLENCY

GEORGE WASHINGTON, Esquire,

GENERAL and COMMANDER in CHIEF of the FORCES
of the UNITED STATES OF AMERICA.

BY Virtue of the Power and Direction to Me efpe-
cially given, I hereby enjoin and require all Perfons
refiding within feventy Miles of my Head Quarters to
threfh one Half of their Grain by the 1ft Day of February,
and the other Half by the 1ft Day of March next enfuing,
on Pain, in Cafe of Failure of having all that fhall re-
main in Sheaves after the Period above mentioned, feized
by the Commiffaries and Quarter-Mafters of the Army,
and paid for as Straw

GIVEN *under my Hand, at Head Quarters, near*
the Valley Forge, in Philadelphia County, *this 20th*
Day of December, 1777.

G. *WASHINGTON.*

By His Excellency's Command,

ROBERT H. HARRISON, Sec'y.

LANCASTER: PRINTED BY JOHN DUNLAP.

In an effort to obtain food, Washington requisitioned supplies from area farmers
with proclamations such as this. He met with little success.

there has been little less than a famine in camp. A part of the army has been a week without any kind of flesh, and the rest three or four days."

The situation was particularly galling and infuriating because the general population was reasonably well off and well fed. A recent exile from Philadelphia, Christopher Marshall, wrote bitterly, "Our affairs wear a very gloomy aspect. Great part of our army gone into winter quarters . . . wanting breeches, shoes, stockings, blankets, and . . . in want of flour, yet being in a land of plenty, our farmers having their barns and barracks full of grain, hundreds of barrels of flour lying on the banks of the Susquehanna perishing for want to care in securing it from the weather. . . ." The sad truth was that while many citizens supported the rebellion against the British in theory, few were willing to support it in a way that might cost them money.

To avoid a possible mutiny in the army, foraging parties were set up to obtain food from nearby farms. Joseph was chosen for one of these parties.

A foraging party would approach a farmer and offer to buy livestock, grain, or vegetables with Continental dollars. If the farmer refused, the items would be requisitioned (by force if necessary) and the money left behind.

Most farmers, even those sympathetic to the American cause, were not eager to accept Continental dollars. In January, 1777, it took $105 in Continental currency to equal $100 in gold; one year later, the value of a Continental dollar had fallen so much that it took 325 of them to equal $100 in gold. And by April of 1780, you had to have four thousand Continental dollars to get $100 in gold. Joseph summed up the popular feeling about the new currency when he said, "Continental money [is] worth about as much as its weight in rags."

It is little wonder he was uneasy about being part of a foraging party. Foraging was "nothing more nor less than *procuring* provisions from the inhabitants . . . at the point of the bayonet. I could not, while in the very act of taking their cattle, hay, corn and grain from them against their

Continental money "was only a promise to pay, and the promise was not worth much." Farmers preferred to sell their crops to the British, who paid in gold.

wills, consider it a whit better than plundering—sheer privateering."

But Joseph understood the need for foraging. "We were now absolutely in danger of perishing, and that too, in the midst of a plentiful country. Had there fallen deep snows or even heavy and long rainstorms . . . or had the enemy . . . thought fit to pursue us, our poor emaciated carcasses *would* have 'strewed the plain.'"

Under the direction of a corporal, Joseph and five other men rode out of camp one morning. To accent the miserable condition of the army and its need for supplies, the last sentry they passed was barefoot and standing on his hat to keep his feet off the cold, hard ground.

Whatever guilty feelings Joseph had when he left camp were soon overcome when he learned about the important benefits that went along with his new job. "Some of us were constantly in the country with the wagons; we went out by turns and had no one to control us. Our lieuten-

Even when food was obtained, the supply wagons had to contend with snow- and ice-covered roads.

ant scarcely ever saw us or we him. Our sergeant never went out with us once, all the time we were there. . . ."

More important than escaping the eyes of bossy officers, foraging also gave Joseph a chance to fill his belly. "When we were in the country we were pretty sure to fare well, for the inhabitants were remarkably kind to us."

Once, while stopping at a tavern, he discovered that he and the landlord had the same last name. "He had a son about my age, whose given name was the same as mine. This son was taken prisoner at Fort Lee in the year 1776, and died on his way home. These good people were almost willing to persuade themselves that I was their son. . . . I fared none the worse for my name [and] I often wished afterwards that I could find more namesakes."

These pleasant times lasted nearly four months, when Joseph was told to rejoin his company at Valley Forge. Immediately on his return, he noticed a difference in the other men. Spirits were surprisingly high. First, American forces under General Horatio Gates had recaptured Saratoga, New York, in late October and had eliminated the British threat to Albany and much of the north. Then in February, France had declared war on Britain and promised to support the American cause with troops and supplies. But the most obvious change was in the way they drilled: lines were perfectly straight and when orders were shouted, the men turned sharply and with precision.

While Joseph was out foraging, Baron Friedrich von Steuben had arrived at Valley Forge and volunteered to serve on Washington's staff. Steuben, a veteran of European wars, was a Prussian citizen who knew little English besides a few well-chosen curses. Washington was impressed by the Baron's military credentials, but more so by his belief in the American cause. "The object of my greatest ambition," the baron told Washington, "is to render your country all the services in my power to deserve the title of a citizen of America by fighting for the cause of your liberty." Washington took him on, assigning him the chore of drilling the troops.

A young Frenchman, Marie Joseph Paul Yves Roch Gilbert du Motier, is better known to us as the Marquis de Lafayette. When Lafayette joined the American forces he had no military experience, but he quickly became an accomplished and brave officer.

Baron Friedrich von Steuben showed up at Valley Forge as an unpaid volunteer who spoke little English. Still, he managed to simplify the drill manual and had American troops marching crisply in a matter of weeks.

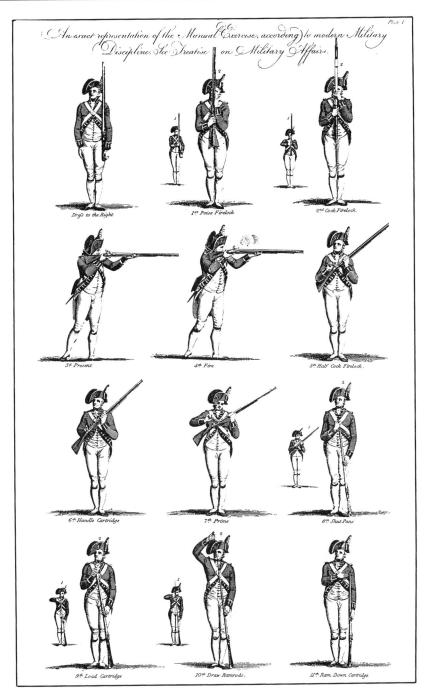

An eighteenth-century engraving demonstrates the proper way a British soldier was to load a musket (positions 6 through 11) and fire it (positions 3 and 4).

The first thing Steuben did was simplify the drill manual and make all orders uniform. Up to this time the wording for commands varied from company to company. An officer might follow the manual of arms used by the British, but the more independent-minded and creative ones simply made up their own. Next Steuben took one hundred soldiers and drilled them tirelessly until they had the snap and precision of regulars. These one hundred soldiers were then sent to train other parts of the army and so on and on. When the warm weather arrived in 1778, the amateur army had been transformed into a disciplined organization—and soldiers like Joseph had to catch up.

"After I had rejoined my regiment I was kept constantly, when off other duty, engaged in learning the Baron de Steuben's new Prussian exercise. It was a continual drill."

And, of course, there was the usual matter of food. During the winter he had found plenty to eat, but now "I had to enter again on my old system of starving." On good days he might be given eight or ten ounces of beef or a turnip, or he might find some nuts or berries while on patrol. Most days he had to content himself with something called a "fire cake."

To make this, he mixed flour and water and shaped it into a flat patty. Then he slapped the tasteless dough onto a hot rock sitting in the fire's embers and grilled the patty dark brown on both sides. It wasn't a very satisfying or nutritious meal, but it did stop his stomach from growling, at least for a while.

Late in May, rumors began to spread throughout the American troops—the British were planning to abandon Philadelphia. The American victory at Saratoga, coupled with their war with France, had worried the British high command much more than Washington or Congress realized. They feared that a French fleet of ships would sail up the Delaware River and trap the British troops there. The decision was made to consolidate British troops in New York where the British fleet was stationed and where there was ready access to the sea.

On June 18th nearly ten thousand British soldiers, along with several thousand Philadelphia citizens loyal to the crown and fifteen hundred wagons of their household belongings, began the slow journey across New Jersey. The dirt roads in the area were narrow and in very poor condition, so the retreating British forces were strung out single file in a column several miles long. Heavy rains fell and the marching feet churned the road into ankle-deep mud. As they struggled north, American snipers picked away at them mercilessly. To further delay the British, Washington had men burn the bridges along the route and cut down trees to block the road.

When the rain stopped, 96-degree heat and humidity took over. Their thick wool uniforms, sixty-pound packs, and heavy muskets caused hundreds of British to fall victim to sunstroke and heat prostration. They were making just four miles a day when they stumbled into a tiny town named Monmouth Court House and called a halt.

Joseph was in a detachment of one thousand men trailing the redcoats closely, though they did little more than tour the back roads and country towns at first. In Princeton, "some of the patriotic inhabitants of the town brought out . . . casks of ready-made toddy. It was dealt out to the men as they passed by, which caused the detachment to move slowly at this place. The young ladies of the town . . . were sitting in the stoops and at the windows to see the noble exhibition of a thousand half-starved and three-quarters naked soldiers pass in review before them."

Spring had once again swollen the ranks of the American army. Washington now had 13,500 men under his command, giving him a clear advantage over the enemy. He had all his troops converge on Monmouth, with orders to attack when the British began to march again. Unfortunately, American general Charles Lee and the six thousand troops he commanded blundered right into the main force of the British, who were dug in and waiting.

Lee was Washington's senior officer and had opposed the idea of fighting the British at Monmouth. "We cannot stand against them," he had told Washington. He was so reluctant to engage the British that he didn't even formulate a plan of action for his troops when the fighting began.

Lee was stunned by the size of the British forces he faced, but instead of directing his now well-trained troops into position, he got into an argument with one of his junior officers. They exchanged angry words for nearly an hour, during which time only a tiny part of Lee's force actually did any fighting.

At about this time, Joseph's group was drawing near the scene. "We went in a road running through a deep narrow valley, which was covered with thick woods. . . . While in the wood we heard a volley or two of musketry. . . ."

They left the cool shade of the trees and entered a broad field. "The sun shining full upon the field, the soil of which was sandy, the mouth of a heated oven seemed to me to be but a trifle hotter than this ploughed field; it was almost impossible to breathe."

Desperate hand-to-hand fighting at Monmouth.

The men were positioned in a straight row, ready to fire on any British who came their way. An officer moved along the lines saying, "Now you have been wishing for some days past to come up with the British, you have been waiting to fight—now you shall have fighting enough. . . ."

Joseph knelt, his musket cocked and ready, beads of sweat running down his face and stinging his eyes. Then for no apparent reason "we received orders to retreat, as all the left wing of the army, that part being under the command of General Lee, were retreating. Grating as this order was to our feelings, we were obliged to comply."

After finishing his battlefield argument with his junior officer, Lee began ordering various companies to new positions. Since he didn't bother to explain his plans to anyone, his officers and the men under them assumed he had called retreat.

Joseph's group pulled back into the trees and waited near a muddy brook. While here, General Washington came galloping up and "I heard him ask our officers 'by whose order the troops were retreating,' and being answered, 'by General Lee's,' he said something [but] he was too far off for me to hear it distinctly. Those that were nearer to him said that his words were 'd——n him.' Whether he did thus express himself or not I do not know. It was certainly very unlike him, but he seemed at the instant to be in a great passion; his looks if not his words seemed to indicate as much."

Washington rode to the open field and watched as the enemy approached. "He remained there some time upon his old English charger, while the shot from the British artillery were rending up the earth all around him. After he had taken a view of the enemy, he returned and ordered [a brigade] to make a stand at a fence. . . ."

Next, Washington hurried to position troops and artillery and get them ready for a counterattack. On command his soldiers turned and reformed their lines just as Steuben had taught them. General Lee came along about then and Washington relieved him of his command and ordered him off the battlefield. With Washington in complete command, the real Battle of Monmouth commenced.

An angry George Washington relieves General Charles Lee of command and halts the retreat of American soldiers.

The British drove off the defenders near the fence and "planted their cannon upon the place and began a violent attack upon [our] artillery and detachment." The exchange of cannon fire went on for nearly half an hour, but, as a proud Joseph noted, "neither could be routed."

It was during this duel that Joseph noticed a woman helping to load one of the big guns. "While in the act of reaching [for] a cartridge and having one of her feet as far before the other as she could step, a cannon shot from the enemy passed directly between her legs without doing any other damage than carrying away all the lower part of her petticoat. Looking at it with apparent unconcern, she observed that it was lucky it did not pass a little higher. . . ." The woman's name was Mary Ludwig Hayes and she, like many wives, had followed her husband into battle, only to join the fight after several artillerymen were wounded. Today, she is better known as Molly Pitcher.

One by one the British cannon were disabled and the enemy "reluctantly crawled back . . . and hid themselves from our sight. . . . We instantly marched towards the enemy's right wing, which was in the orchard, and kept concealed from them as long as possible by keeping behind the bushes. [Then] we marched into the open fields and formed our line. The British immediately formed and began to retreat to the main body of their army."

After her husband was wounded, Molly Pitcher manned his position at the cannon during the Battle of Monmouth.

This must have been a thrilling sight for the American troops, to see hundreds of redcoats, or lobsterbacks as soldiers from Maine referred to them, scurrying for safety. The enemy soldiers were just entering a meadow and the officer in charge of the Connecticut troops called out: "Come, my boys, reload your pieces, and we will give them a set-off."

"They were retreating in line, though in some disorder" Joseph recalled. "I singled out a man and took my aim directly between his shoulders (they were divested of their packs); he was a good mark, being a broad-shouldered fellow, but what became of him I know not; the fire and smoke hid him from my sights. One thing I know . . . I took as deliberate aim at him as ever I did at any game in my life. . . ."

After giving them "the parting salute," Joseph added, "the firing on both sides ceased. We then laid ourselves down under the fences and

American soldiers break from the line of march to scoop up precious drops of water.

bushes to take a breath, for we had need of it. . . . Fighting is hot work in cool weather, how much more so in such weather as it was on the twenty-eighth of June, 1778."

While the fighting in Joseph's area was over, the retreat did not signal the end of the battle. Pockets of musket and cannon fire erupted all through the afternoon and well into the evening. In places, the British pushed the Americans back, but overall, the forces under Washington held their ground. At one point, the British threw their best troops, the famous Black Guard, against a line of Americans. Eyewitnesses claim that Washington beamed with pride and Steuben cursed happily in several languages as the Americans stood firm and traded volley for volley until the enemy withdrew. At midnight, the British packed up their gear, quietly withdrew from the battlefield, and hurried to the safety of New York.

After a much-needed night of rest, Joseph and the rest of the men in his group awoke and received a reward for their valiant fighting. "Each man received a gill [one-quarter pint] of rum, but nothing to eat." They then marched off to surround the British in New York.

While neither side came away from Monmouth with a decisive victory, Washington had the most to be pleased about. His soldiers had stood up to the British on the open field and proved they were a unified fighting force. In addition, as Washington observed, "It is not a little pleasing, nor less wonderful to contemplate that, after two years Manoeuvring . . . both Armies are brought back to the very point they set out from."

No one realized it at the time, but Monmouth marked a turning point in the Revolution. This was the last major battle to take place north of the Delaware. The British would soon all but give up on holding the northern states and, instead, set their sights on the South.

Even though fighting slackened off following Monmouth, the work of a Continental soldier did not. Here eight men struggle to haul a cannon up a steep trail.

CHAPTER SIX

The War and Joseph Go South

The British decision to give up the New England states did not mean fighting stopped in the North. English soldiers still occupied New York City and patrols were sent out into the surrounding states on a regular basis.

Most of Joseph's days were taken up with marching—through the woods of Connecticut and Rhode Island, into the mountainous regions of New York State, and down into the sandy, flat areas of New Jersey. At one point he was sent with about two hundred other soldiers to Westfield, New Jersey. "We were stationed about six miles from Elizabethtown, which is situated near the waters which separate Staten Island from the main. We had another guard . . . at a place called Woodbridge; and this was ten miles from our quarters. . . . Our duty all the winter and spring was [to march between] Woodbridge and Elizabethtown, Elizabethtown and Woodbridge, alternately, till I was absolutely sick of hearing the names mentioned."

There were still encounters with the British, but they were growing less and less frequent. One problem that never went away was hostility from citizens loyal to the King. One out of every three citizens Joseph encountered still sided with the Crown and some towns seemed to have more Loyalists than others. Woodbridge teemed with British sympathizers, at least according to Joseph. "There was no trusting the inhabitants, for many of them were friendly to the British, and we did not know who were or who were not, and consequently, were distrustful of them all. . . ."

At this stage of the war, Loyalists rarely confronted American soldiers directly. Usually they confined their anti-Patriot activities to spying, reporting American troop movements and strengths, or pinpointing the location of campsites. Joseph did have one close call.

He was in Rhode Island on patrol with a small group of soldiers. They stopped at a house beside a river and were having a pleasant chat with the owner when Joseph noticed a house on an island about a quarter-mile away. There was a large group of men on the island, but "as they appeared to be a motley group, I did not pay them much attention."

Joseph was just finishing his conversation when "I saw the flash of a gun. I instinctively dropped, as quick as a loon could dive, when the ball passed directly over me and lodged in the tree under which [I was] standing. . . . The people [on the island] set up a shouting, thinking they had done the job for one poor Yankee, but they were mistaken, for I immediately rose up, and slapping my backsides to them, slowly moved off. . . ."

Despite instances like this, the most troublesome aspect of being a soldier in the Revolution was still the shortage of supplies, especially food. "Our duty was not quite so hard now as it had been, but that faithful companion, hunger, stuck as close to us as ever." It could be said that while British regulars could not defeat the Americans, the lack of food nearly did.

The winter of 1779 and 1780 was easily the harshest of the Revolution. Early in November a severe snowstorm blanketed the northeast, followed by a hard frost that killed the vine crops. American troops arrived at their winter camp at Jockey Hollow, about three miles from Morristown, and were greeted with a blizzard before they could even build their cabins.

The snow blocked the roads, halting the movement of the few supply wagons in the area. The wind and snow blinded anyone who ventured outside and often tore apart the hastily pitched tents. When the snow stopped, the temperature plummeted, producing a bone-chilling cold.

Joseph huddled in his tent, his one blanket wrapped around his shoulders. Outside his flimsy shelter the wind howled; inside, his stomach growled. "We were absolutely literally starved. I do solemnly declare that I did not put a morsel of victuals into my mouth for four days and as many nights, except a little black-birch bark which I gnawed off a stick of wood, if that can be called victuals. I saw several of the men roast their old shoes and eat them, and I was afterwards informed . . . that some of the officers killed and ate a favorite little dog that belonged to one of them. If this was not 'suffering' I request to be informed what can pass under the name."

Some food did make it to the troops, mainly through the generosity of citizens from nearby towns. But there was never enough to satisfy the soldiers' hunger or their feeling that the American Congress and people had abandoned them. Even as the warmer weather of spring arrived, supplies remained shamefully inadequate.

Throughout the war, American soldiers staged mutinies to show their discontent and impatience. Most of these were poorly organized, did not involve large numbers of soldiers, and did not disrupt the day-to-day operations of the army. Following the winter at Morristown, the mutinies grew in size and anger. The problem was so serious that Washington told Congress that the low morale of his troops "has given me infinitely more concern than any thing that has ever happened."

Joseph was a part of two mutinies staged by Connecticut soldiers, a small one that was quickly resolved in 1779 and a much more serious one in 1780. Because officers did not want to encourage other soldiers to mutiny, or let the enemy know such problems existed, they did not write in much detail about these incidents. In fact, Joseph's narrative provides the longest and most detailed account known of a mutiny among the Continental troops.

As he remembers, it was May, 1780, and "we got a little musty bread and a little beef, about every other day, but this lasted only a short time and then we got nothing at all. The men were now exasperated beyond endurance; they could not stand it any longer. They saw no other alterna-

The prison ship Jersey *looks harmless enough moored near Long Island, but conditions were foul and inhumane. Historian Lawrence H. Leder estimates that as many as eleven thousand soldiers died while imprisoned here—more than were killed in actual fighting.*

tive but to starve to death, or break up the army, give all up and go home. This was a hard matter for the soldiers to think upon. They were truly patriotic, they loved their country, and they had already suffered everything short of death in its cause; and now, after such extreme hardships to give up all was too much, but to starve to death was too much also. What was to be done? Here was the army starved and naked, and there their country sitting still and expecting the army to do notable things while fainting from sheer starvation. All things considered, the army was not to be blamed."

Trouble began brewing on a particularly pleasant spring day. While parading along the countryside, the men spent a great deal of time "growling like sorehead dogs. At evening roll call they began to show their dissatisfaction by snapping at the officers and acting contrary to their orders." The soldiers were looking for trouble, so when an officer called one of them a "mutinous rascal" this man stamped "the butt of his musket upon the ground, as much as to say, I am in a passion, [and then he] called out 'Who will parade with me?' The whole regiment immediately fell in and formed."

Joseph's group had no real leader or plan, but they managed to get the drummer to play and then marched off to join up with two other regiments of disgruntled soldiers. Officers ran to the angry soldiers and ordered them to return to their huts. None of the soldiers obeyed and a shouting-match began that ended in a scuffle, during which an officer was injured slightly with a bayonet.

Pennsylvania troops soon arrived and surrounded the mutinous soldiers. "Being informed that [we] had mutinied on account of the scarcity of provisions, 'Let us join them,' said they. 'Let us join the Yankees; they are good fellows, and have no notion of lying here like fools and starving.' Their officers needed no further hinting. The [Pennsylvania] troops were quickly ordered back to their quarters, from fear that they would join in the same song with the Yankees."

Not long after this, the Connecticut officers realized their presence was only making matters worse, so they left. The soldiers continued their protest through the night, "venting our spleen at our country and government, then at our officers, and then at ourselves for our imbecility in staying there and starving . . . for an ungrateful people who did not care what became of us, so they could enjoy themselves while we were keeping a cruel enemy from them."

Finally, a Pennsylvania officer whom the soldiers all respected, Colonel Walter Stewart, came to talk with them. After finding out why they had rebelled, Stewart said, " 'Your officers suffer as much as you do. We all suffer. The officers have no money to purchase supplies with any more than the private men have. . . . I have no other resources than you have to depend upon. I had not a sixpence to purchase a partridge that was offered me the other day. Besides,' said he, 'you know not how much you injure your own characters by such conduct. You Connecticut troops have won immortal honor to yourselves the winter past, by your perseverance, patience, and bravery, and now you are shaking it off at your heels.'"

This little speech seems to have worked. The tempers of the men cooled enough that they began drifting back to their huts, hungry, but satisfied that their officers had finally gotten the message. A day later, provisions arrived, and the soldiers learned that no charges would be brought against them. How could they be punished, Washington would say, when they were in the right?

While Continental forces grumbled and went hungry, they did not lose their spirit or the will to be free of the British. Winters caused many men to give up and go home, but each spring saw new recruits signing on and ready to fight. Meanwhile, one problem after another hit the British. Money and supplies from the French were beginning to strengthen the American rebels. More important, the French fleet cruised the Atlantic, attacking British warships and supply vessels. In 1779 Spain declared war on Britain, followed by the Netherlands in 1780. With wars raging in various parts of Europe, as well as in America, the British military was stretched thin.

In addition, their attempt to subdue the South went badly. After taking both Savannah, Georgia, and then Charleston, South Carolina, easily, the British sent troops into the countryside. They met little real opposition at first. Then large numbers of local partisan fighters joined the Continental forces to battle the invaders. Everywhere the British turned, bands of Americans waited for them. Gradually, the British pulled their troops back to the seacoast towns.

In 1781, the British decided to concentrate on winning Virginia and began moving troops there. Once they had secured Virginia, they reasoned, they could cut off supplies and troops to the area south and subdue it. All spring and summer, British and American troops clashed, though neither side won a decisive victory. In June, Washington began sending some of his northern troops south to reinforce the American forces there. The commander of the British army in the south, General George Cornwallis, moved his entire force of ninety-five hundred men to Yorktown to resupply and prepare for another offensive thrust into the countryside.

While all this was going on, Joseph was promoted to the Corps of Sappers and Miners, a division of the engineer's department. Their main job was to prepare the mines and approach trenches, called the saps, to the enemy's fortifications. They also built the roads, laid out the camps, and scouted the enemy's fortifications in advance of an attack.

Joseph was in the middle of learning his new duties when "we all of a sudden marched." They left New York State, crossing the Hudson into New Jersey, and stopped in Chatham.

At Chatham a field was marked out for an extensive encampment and a number of ovens were erected for the baking of bread. Everyone—soldiers, officers, local citizens, and Loyalist spies—assumed, as Joseph did, that "we were to attack New York [City]."

This is precisely what Washington wanted everyone, especially the British, to think. The truth was that Washington planned to sneak his entire army, along with all of the French soldiers, past the British in New York and hurry them south. If he managed to do this, he would have twenty thousand soldiers in Virginia, more than enough to encircle and trap Cornwallis at Yorktown. Even Joseph was surprised when he was ordered up at four in the morning and marched to Philadelphia. "[There] we found a *large* fleet of *small* vessels waiting to convey us and other troops, stores, &c. down the bay."

When Chatham awoke, the army was gone and no one had a clear idea of where it was headed. The great march of the combined American and French forces had gone exactly as planned. In fact, there would be only two real surprises during the entire time. The first was for all American soldiers. As a startled and delighted Joseph reported, "we each of us received a MONTH'S PAY, in specie, borrowed . . . from the officers in the French army. This was the first that could be called money, which we had received as wages since the year '76, or that we ever did receive till the close of the war. . . ."

The other surprise was for the British. When no Americans attacked

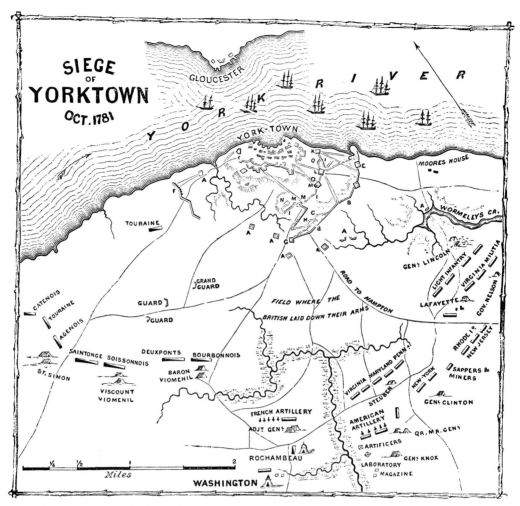

American and French forces form a tight semicircle around Yorktown, while the French fleet controls the waters and cuts off any hope of escape.

New York, they began to suspect that they'd been fooled. A fleet of nineteen ships was sent to rescue the troops at Yorktown, but when they sailed into Chesapeake Bay they found twenty-four French warships waiting for them. The two fleets fired some shots at each other; then the wind died down and they sat watching each other for five days. Twelve more French ships arrived during the lull, and the British saw that they were clearly outnumbered. When the wind once again freshened, the British turned and sailed off.

This Battle of the Chesapeake Capes was one of the most decisive nonfights in history. The French fleet now controlled the bay and coast, while the combined American and French troops encircled the city. The British at Yorktown were completely surrounded and helpless. It did not take long for Cornwallis to learn that there would be no rescue. When he heard the news, he turned away from his officers and shouted, "It is no good! The game is lost!"

Even though there was no way he could win a battle, Cornwallis decided not to surrender. He dug in, hoping to hold off the enemy long enough for a larger British fleet to save him and his army.

Smoke and cannon fire fill the air during the Battle of the Chesapeake Capes. This sea "battle" did end with the French fleet in control of the seas, but there was little actual fighting.

Washington had no intention of giving Cornwallis any time at all. On the night of October 5th, Joseph and the other sappers and miners sneaked to within one hundred fifty feet of the British lines. "It was a very dark and rainy night," he remembered. "We repaired to the place and began by following the engineers and laying laths of pine wood end-to-end upon the line marked out by the officers for the trenches."

A complicated series of trenches was going to be dug to encircle York-town. These trenches would allow hundreds of pieces of artillery and thousands of soldiers to get very close to the British and still have protection. When the wooden outline was in place a tall officer appeared and began talking to the engineers about the work. "They discoursed together some time, when, by the officers calling him 'Your Excellency,' we discovered that it was General Washington. Had we dared, we might have cautioned him for exposing himself too carelessly to danger at such a time. . . ."

Soldiers were moved to the area and given shovels and picks. Before the actual digging began, "General Washington . . . struck a few blows with a pickax . . . that it might be said 'General Washington with his own hands first broke ground at the siege of Yorktown.'"

When the ceremony had ended, the real work began. The ground was sandy and soft, so digging went swiftly. To distract the British, "our people had sent to the western side of [us] a detachment to make a number of fires, by which, and our men passing before the fires, the British were led to imagine that we were about some secret mischief there, and consequently directed their whole fire to that quarter, while we were entrenching literally under their noses."

Of course, as soon as the sun came up, "they perceived their mistake and began firing where they ought to have done sooner. They brought out a fieldpiece or two, . . . and discharged several shots at the men who were at work erecting a bomb battery."

Every time a cannon was fired, a large and ferocious-looking bulldog would scurry out of the British trenches and follow the ball all the way into the American lines. Then it would turn around and hurry home to

This highly imaginative French engraving portrays the Battle of Yorktown as a classic siege of a walled castle. In truth, Yorktown was less a fort than a pretty little town, and the British defenses were scattered and frail.

await the next shot. American officers wanted to catch the dog and attach a message to his collar for his masters, "but he looked too formidable for any of us to encounter."

With cannon fire as a constant companion, the digging went on. There were thousands of feet of trenches to dig, so the work took nine days to complete. Supplies in Yorktown began to run low, and for the first time during the war the British troops were the ones who went hungry. On October 15th, American and French troops and artillery were all in place.

A very nervous Joseph stationed himself in the front trench to watch the beginning of the siege. "All were upon the tiptoe of expectation and impatience to see the signal given, which was to be the hoisting of the

Washington (at center) watches as the bombardment of Yorktown commences.

American flag in the ten-gun battery. About noon the much-wished-for signal went up. I confess I felt a secret pride swell my heart when I saw the 'star-spangled banner' waving majestically in the very faces of our implacable adversaries. . . . A simultaneous discharge of all the guns in the line followed, the French troops accompanying it with 'Huzza for the Americans!'"

American cannons fired at pointblank range, destroying British trenches and artillery and leveling houses in the town. Late in the afternoon of the second day of bombardment Joseph and the other sappers and miners were given new orders. They were issued axes and told that a general charge would take place when the sun set. "[We were] to proceed in front and cut a passage for the troops through the abatis, which are composed of the tops of trees, the small branches cut off with a slanting stroke which renders them sharp as spikes. These trees are then laid at a small distance from the trench or ditch, pointing outwards, and the butts fastened to the ground. . . . It is almost impossible to get through them."

Joseph waited anxiously as darkness slowly came. Then he and the others inched forward as quietly as possible. "Just as we arrived at the abatis, the enemy discovered us and directly opened a sharp fire upon us. . . . The Sappers and Miners soon cleared a passage for the infantry, who entered it rapidly. [We] were ordered not to enter the fort, but there was no stopping [us]."

The entrance that Joseph had hacked open was jammed with American soldiers rushing to get through. He went down the line a little and found a hole blown through by a cannonball. "While passing, a man at my side received a ball in his head and fell under my feet, crying out bitterly. . . . As I mounted the breastwork, I met an old associate hitching himself down into the trench. I knew him by the light of the enemy's musketry, it was so vivid."

Fierce hand-to-hand fighting followed with shouts of "the fort's our own!" and "Rush on boys" as encouragement. A blanket of powder smoke made seeing in the dark nearly impossible, though Joseph did manage to spot "a British soldier jump over the walls of the fort next to the river and go down the bank, which was almost perpendicular and twenty or thirty feet high. When he came to the beach he made off . . . and if he did not make good use of his legs I never saw a man that did."

Soon the shooting and shouting lessened as British soldiers either fled the fort or threw down their weapons to surrender. From the walls of Yorktown, Cornwallis watched the rout for several minutes, then composed a hasty note and had it sent to Washington under a flag of truce. It was the message Washington had been waiting to receive since the war started, five years before. "I request . . . a cessation of hostilities for twenty-four hours . . . to settle . . . terms for surrender."

Two days later, Joseph and the rest of the American and French forces

Following the formal surrender of arms and company colors, Washington sent off a dispatch: "I have the honor to inform Congress, that a reduction of the British Army under the Command of Lord Cornwallis, is most happily effected. . . ."

were lined up on either side of the road leading from Yorktown. The gates to the city were thrown open and British soldiers began filing out, their jaws set, their eyes staring straight ahead. Regimental flags were handed over to American soldiers; then, one at a time, the British stacked their arms in neat piles and left the open field under guard. They were no longer the enemy; they were prisoners of war. As they marched away an English band played music. The title of the song was "The World Turned Upside Down."

CHAPTER SEVEN

Parted Forever

The American-French victory at Yorktown broke the fighting spirit of the British and signaled the beginning of the end. But like most wars, the conflict did not end immediately. The King of England, George III, simply could not see that fighting to hold onto the colonies was useless. On hearing about Yorktown, he declared that no one should think that it "makes the smallest alteration in those principles of my conduct which have directed me in past time." He insisted, as he had done all along, that "when once these rebels have felt a smart blow, they will submit; and no situation can ever change my fixed resolution to bring the colonies to due obedience. . . ." He ordered the British forces remaining in America to fight on as best they could.

Besides twelve thousand troops in New York, the British had several garrisons scattered throughout the South. Washington had no other choice but to divide up his forces, leaving half in the South to contain the enemy there while moving the rest of his soldiers back to New York.

Joseph was a part of the army that went north. There was very little actual fighting going on, so he spent most of his time doing chores around camp or carrying out special assignments. In November of 1781, he was put in charge of two men and assigned the task of bringing back a deserter who had fled into the New Jersey countryside.

"As [we were] in the vicinity of the place where I had passed the winter of 1779–80, I was acquainted with several of the inhabitants in the neighborhood, and accordingly, sent one of my men to a house hard by, the master of which I knew to be a fine man." On hearing that Joseph was nearby, the man invited him and the other two soldiers to stay the night. "We had a good warm room to sit and lodge in, and as the next day was Thanksgiving, we had an excellent supper." Joseph did not list all of the food he ate, but it was a far cry from the Thanksgiving of 1777, when Congress ordered a "Continental Thanksgiving." Back then, Joseph's holiday meal consisted of a tablespoon of vinegar (which was a standard cure for scurvy) and a quarter cup of rice.

The next day, the man urged Joseph and his men to stay for a leisurely breakfast of "buckwheat slapjacks, flowing with butter and honey, and a capital dish of chocolate." They enjoyed this meal so much that they stayed for lunch, and then dinner. In the end, they lingered in the area for nearly two weeks, going from farmhouse to farmhouse and meal to meal, and never did catch the deserter.

Eventually, Joseph was sent to New York, where the sappers and miners built barracks at West Point. 1782 ended with snowstorms blanketing the North and 1783 began with a visit from an old friend: hunger. Once again, Congress was so broke it could not afford to feed its own army. Conditions became so unbearable that even the officers threatened to mutiny this time. "The temper of the army," Washington warned a member of the Congress, "is much soured and has become more irritable than at any period since the commencement of the war."

Then in the spring of 1783, the King at last realized the bleak reality of the situation he faced—to commit so many British troops to North America opened England to direct invasion from his European enemies. On April 15th, a provisional peace treaty was signed with his rebellious American subjects. After eight long and desperate years of fighting, the colonies were granted their freedom from Great Britain, and the United States of America was born.

A jubilant and proud George Washington would exclaim, "For it will not be believed that such a force as Great Britain has employed for eight years in this Country could be baffled in their plan for Subjugating it by

The parade of the Continental Army as it enters New York.

numbers infinitely less, composed of Men oftentimes half starved; always in Rags, without pay, and experiencing, at times, every species of distress which human nature is capable of undergoing."

Joseph, along with most other soldiers in the Continental Army, received the news with decidedly mixed feelings. They were delighted and joyous that "the war was over and the prize won for which we had been contending through eight tedious years." But there was another troubling feeling also at work and the soldiers did very little celebrating.

"Their chief thoughts were more closely fixed upon their situation as it respected the figure they were to exhibit upon leaving the army, becoming citizens. Starved, ragged and meager, not a cent to help themselves with, and no means or method in view to remedy or alleviate their condition. This was appalling in the extreme. All that they could do was to make a virtue of necessity and face the threatening evils with the same resolution

In November, 1783, the Continental Army was officially disbanded, and the soldiers went home.

and fortitude that they had for so long a time faced the enemy in the field."

Washington tried to get three months' back pay for his men, but Congress did not grant his request, claiming it could not afford the expense. It offered the troops certificates that promised they would be paid when money was available, and let the men keep their arms. Many soldiers, Joseph among them, were forced to sell both the certificates and their weapons "to procure decent clothing and money sufficient to enable them to pass with decency through the country and to appear something like themselves when they arrived among their friends."

Joseph and thousands of other soldiers were officially released from the army on June 11th. "Some of the soldiers went off for home the same day that their fetters were knocked off," he remembered. He lingered several days, reliving his many adventures and narrow escapes with his friends, and enjoying the fact that he no longer had to take orders from anyone. But at last came his day to leave.

"I confess, after all, that my anticipation of the happiness I should experience upon such a day as this was not realized; I can assure the reader that there was as much sorrow as joy transfused on the occasion. We had lived together as a family of brothers for several years, setting aside some little family squabbles, like most other families, had shared with each other the hardships, dangers, and sufferings incident to a soldier's life; had sympathized with each other in trouble and sickness; had assisted in bearing each other's burdens or strove to make them lighter by counsel and advice; had endeavored to conceal each other's faults or make them appear in as good a light as they would bear. . . . And now we were to be . . . parted forever; as unconditionally separated as though the grave lay between us. . . . We were young men and had warm hearts. I question if there was a corps in the army that parted with more regret than ours did. . . ."

The war was over, the victory and liberty won. On a warm summer afternoon, Joseph shouldered a pack containing his few provisions and began his long walk home and into the future.

Nearly one hundred years after the war, the image of the American soldier has been polished to a romantic glow. He is well fed and wears a clean, new uniform. It's doubtful that Joseph Plumb Martin would have recognized this man as a fellow soldier.

CHAPTER EIGHT

A Cordial and Long Farewell

After his discharge from the army, the now twenty-two-year-old Joseph had to begin his life anew as an adult. He spent several months teaching the children of Dutch farmers in upstate New York, but eventually migrated to an unsettled section of Maine near a town that would eventually be called Prospect.

The area was wilderness in the eighteenth century, and land was being offered at low prices to encourage settlers to move there. Joseph farmed the rocky soil as well as he could and married Lucy Clewley, the daughter of a neighboring farmer, in 1794. Lucy and Joseph would have five children, one of whom suffered some sort of physical or mental illness. To supplement his meager income, Joseph also served as a town clerk.

Sadly, Joseph did not prosper, and debts mounted. In 1818, Congress enacted a bill to help needy Revolutionary War veterans and Joseph applied for a pension of $8 a month. He was fifty-eight years old and must have felt great shame when he had to admit, "I have no real or personal estate, nor any income whatever, my necessary bedding and wearing apparel excepted, except two cows, six sheep, one pig. I am a laborer, but by reason of age and infirmity I am unable to work. My wife is sickly and rheumatic [and] I have five children. . . . Without my pension I am unable to support myself and family." After some investigation, the review court ruled that his total property was worth just $52 and awarded him the pension.

Whatever hardships Joseph suffered, they did not slow him down or dim his spirit. He read extensively, made detailed sketches of wild birds (some of which still survive), and wrote many short verses. In 1830, when he was seventy years old, he published his account of his years in the Revolutionary War. He was quick to point out that he was not writing a history of the war, but rather a personal recollection of it from his point of view. To make this clear, he titled his book *A Narrative of Some of the Adventures, Dangers and Sufferings of a Revolutionary Soldier, Interspersed with Anecdotes of Incidents that Occurred Within His Own Observation*. His book did not draw much attention at the time, but historians today view it as one of the most detailed and important accounts of the War for Independence.

Even as Joseph approached his ninetieth birthday and blindness darkened his world, he retained much of his vitality and could still spin a spirited story about his many exploits.

At the end of his book, Joseph wrote these parting words: "I will come to a close and trespass upon your time no longer, time that may, doubtless, be spent to more advantage than reading the 'Adventures and Sufferings' of a private soldier. But if you have been really desirous to hear a part, and a part only, of the hardships . . . of that army that achieved our Independence, I can say I am sorry you have not had an abler pen than mine. . . . And now, kind reader, I bid you a cordial and long farewell."

Joseph Plumb Martin died in May of 1850 and was buried a little upriver from his first farm. Years later, the town of Prospect erected a monument at the grave of its most notable citizen. Chiseled into the hard stone is a simple epitaph and one Joseph would have been proud of: "A Soldier of the Revolution."

Bibliography

☆ ☆ ☆ ☆ ☆

Alden, John Richard. *The American Revolution: 1775–1783*. New York: Harper and Brothers Publishers, 1954.

Anonymous. *Advice to the Officers of the British Army: With Some Hints to the Drummer and Private Soldier*. London: Richardson, 1783.

Bakeless, John. *Turncoats, Traitors and Heroes*. Philadelphia: J. B. Lippincott Company, 1959.

Billias, George Athan. *George Washington's Generals*. New York: William Morrow and Company, 1964.

Bliven, Bruce. *Battle For Manhattan*. New York: Henry Holt and Company, 1955.

Bolton, Charles Knowles. *The Private Soldier Under Washington*. Williamstown, MA: Corner House Publishers, 1976.

Busch, Noel F. *Winter Quarters: George Washington and the Continental Army at Valley Forge*. New York: Liveright, 1974.

Chidsey, Donald Barr. *Valley Forge*. New York: Crown Publishers, 1959.

———. *Victory at Yorktown*. New York: Crown Publishers, 1962.

Commager, Henry Steele and Richard B. Morris. *The Spirit of 'Seventy-Six: The Story of the American Revolution as Told by the Participants*, Vol. 1 and 2. Indianapolis: The Bobbs-Merrill Company, 1958.

Cooke, Donald E. *Our Nation's Great Heritage*. Maplewood, NJ: Hammond, 1972.

Dann, John C., ed. *The Revolution Remembered: Eyewitness Accounts of the War for Independence.* Chicago: The University of Chicago Press, 1977.

Davidson, Philip. *Propaganda and the American Revolution: 1763–1783.* Chapel Hill, NC: The University of North Carolina Press, 1941.

Dorson, Richard M. *American Rebels.* New York: Pantheon Books, 1953.

Dring, Captain Thomas. *Recollections of the Jersey Prison Ship.* New York: Corinth Books, 1961.

Dupuy, R. Ernest, Gay Hammerman, and Grace P. Hayes. *The American Revolution: A Global War.* New York: David McKay Company, 1877.

Fleming, Thomas J. *Beat the Last Drum: The Siege of Yorktown, 1781.* New York: St. Martins Press, 1963.

Gelb, Norman. *Less Than Glory.* New York: G. P. Putnam's Sons, 1984.

Greenman, Jeremiah. *Diary of a Common Soldier in the American Revolution, 1775–1783.* DeKalb, IL: Northern Illinois University Press, 1978.

Hibbert, Christopher. *Redcoats and Rebels: The American Revolution Through British Eyes.* New York: W. W. Norton and Company, 1990.

Langguth, A. J. *Patriots: The Men Who Started the American Revolution.* New York: Simon and Schuster, 1988.

Leckie, Robert. *George Washington's War: The Saga of the American Revolution.* New York: HarperCollins Publishers, 1992.

Martin, Joseph Plumb. *A Narrative of Some of the Adventures, Dangers and Sufferings of a Revolutionary Soldier.* Hallowell, ME: Privately printed, 1830.

McDowell, Bart. *The Revolutionary War.* Washington, DC: The National Geographic Society, 1967.

Moore, Frank. *The Diary of the American Revolution: From Newspapers and Original Documents.* Hartford, CT: J. B. Burr and Company, 1876.

——. *Songs and Ballads of the American Revolution.* New York: Appleton and Company, 1856.

Morris, Richard B. *The Forging of the Union: 1781–1789.* New York: Harper and Row, Publishers, 1987.

Nell, William C. *The Colored Patriots of the American Revolution.* Boston: R. F. Wallcut, 1855.

Scheer, George F. and Hugh F. Rankin. *Rebels and Redcoats: The American Revolution Through the Eyes of Those Who Fought and Lived It.* New York: World Publishing Company, 1957.

Schouler, James. *Americans of 1776: Daily Life in Revolutionary America.* Williamstown, MA: Corner House Publishers, 1976.

Stokesbury, James L. *A Short History of the American Revolution.* New York: William Morrow and Company, 1991.

Utley, Beverly, Allan Keller, Ebenezer Fletcher, and Hugh McDonald. *The Uncommon Soldier of the Revolution: Women and Young People who Fought for American Independence.* Yorktown, VA: Eastern Acorn Press, 1986.

Werstein, Irving. *1776: The Adventures of the American Revolution Told Through Pictures.* New York: Cooper Square Publishers, 1962.

White, Donald Wallace. *A Village at War: Chatham, New Jersey, and the American Revolution.* Rutherford, NJ: Fairleigh Dickinson University Press, 1979.

Wright, Robert K. *The Continental Army.* Washington, DC: Center for Military History, United States Army, 1989.

Young, Alfred F. and Terry J. Fife. *We the People: Voices and Images of the New Nation.* Philadelphia: Temple University Press, 1993.

A Brief Chronology
of the American Revolution

1760 — Joseph Plumb Martin is born

1765 — The Stamp Act is passed by Parliament

— "Sons of Liberty" is formed to resist the Stamp Act

1766 — The Stamp Act is repealed

1767 — The Townshend Acts are passed to tax tea, wine, oil, lead, and paint

1769 — All Townshend Acts are repealed except the tax on tea

1770 — The "Boston Massacre" takes place

1772 — British revenue cutter, the *Gaspee,* is burned in Rhode Island

1773 — The "Boston Tea Party" is staged

1774 — British government closes Boston Harbor to all shipping

— First Continental Congress meets in Philadelphia

1775 — British declare that Massachusetts is in a state of rebellion

— Battles of Lexington and Concord take place on April 19th

— Second Continental Congress meets to appoint George Washington commander of the army. Issues call for 20,000 volunteers

— Fort Ticonderoga is captured under the leadership of Benedict Arnold and Ethan Allen

— Americans lose the Battle of Bunker Hill on June 17th

— American attack on Quebec fails

1776 — British evacuate Boston in March

— Declaration of Independence adopted by Congress, July 4th

— Joseph Plumb Martin enlists in Connecticut militia, July 6th

— British drive Americans from Long Island, August 27th

— Battle of Harlem Heights takes place in September

— Battle of White Plains is fought, October 28th

— British capture Fort Washington and take 3000 prisoners, November 16th

— Americans abandon Fort Lee, November 20th

— Washington directs surprise attack on Trenton and captures 1000 Hessian mercenaries, December 26th

1777 — Americans win Battle of Princeton, January 3rd

— Joseph Plumb Martin reenlists in Continental Army in April

— British retake Fort Ticonderoga, July 5th

— British army lands at Elkton, Maryland, August 25th

— Americans defeated at Battle of Brandywine, September 11th

— British occupy Philadelphia, September 26th

— Battle of Germantown takes place, October 4th

— British General Burgoyne surrenders at Saratoga, October 17th

— British evacuate Ticonderoga, November 8th

— Fort Mifflin and Fort Mercer are captured by British, November 15th

— Americans establish winter camp at Valley Forge, December 19th

1778 — France and America sign alliance and France declares war on Great Britain, February 6th

— Americans leave Valley Forge, June 19th

— Battle of Monmouth takes place, June 28th

— British occupy Savannah, Georgia, December 29th

1779 — Spain declares war against Great Britain, May 8th

— British attack the coasts of Virginia and Connecticut

— Americans under General Anthony Wayne capture Stony Point, New York

— John Paul Jones sails to Britain in *Bonhomme Richard* and captures British man-of-war *Serapis* in September

— Combined French and American forces fail to recapture Savannah, October 9th

1780 — Siege of Charleston ends with British victory, May 12th

— French troops arrive to support Washington's army, July 11th

— American General Gates is defeated at Camden, New Jersey, August 16th

— Benedict Arnold deserts to British, September 25th

— Americans defeat British at King's Mountain, North Carolina, October 7th

— The Netherlands declares war on Britain

1781 — Benedict Arnold returns to America and strikes at southern strongholds in January

— British lose at Cowpens, South Carolina, January 17th

— Cornwallis moves his forces to Yorktown, Virginia in August

— French fleet enters Chesapeake Bay, September

— British suffer defeat at Eutaw Springs, South Carolina, September 8th

— Washington takes American army south to besiege Yorktown, September 8th

— Cornwallis surrenders, October 19th

1782 — Holland recognizes the United States, April 19th

— General Anthony Wayne beats British in Georgia, July

— British evacuate Charleston and Savannah in July

— British sign preliminary peace terms with America in November

1783 — Congress declares an end to the war, April 11th

— Last British troops evacuate New York in November, and American troops under George Washington enter the city in triumph

Index

☆ ☆ ☆ ☆ ☆

Italic page numbers refer to illustrations and/or captions.